The Invisible Temple, by Peter Roch
in the development, generation, a
Nowhere will you find more explicit
and use this energy.

D1554481

What is the Invisible Temple? It is not a building or location. It is not a particular congregation of people. It *is* wherever there is a focal point for spiritual energy. It is located where that energy is generated, amplified and transformed for whatever purpose is needed. In other words, when each of us *becomes* an individual spiritual light generator.

It teaches how anyone can be more alive and more conscious, and how he can perfect his potentials by creating "an Energy, Consciousness and Light Generator, Transformer and Amplifier." It shows that all the materials needed are contained in one's own being, or—if available—that of a group of people.

The key to Spiritual Awakening and Understanding is to be found in the expansion of one's consciousness and in personal transformation. The technique involves the directed movement of visualized Light, Warmth, and Vibrations drawn from our own psycho-spiritual centers to awaken the Spiritual Level.

It is the Divine Spark in use which, awakened in our Consciousness, becomes the "officiating priest" (the only valid Initiator) in Spiritual Attainment.

This book instructs on the essential techniques of Meditation, Visualizing the Aura, Energizing the Tree of Life on the Person and the Group, and Living Theurgically teaches practical magical and occult techniques for Spiritual Attainment within a largely Christian framework (but with constant reference to other traditions to show the universality of the techniques themselves).

At the same time, the structure of the Work is Qabalistic, and Christian Symbols and Rituals were actually drawn from a Qabalistic Tradition. The Qabalah is "our own indigenous Western Esoteric Tradition which is most suitable for our CONTEMPORARY way of Life."

The absolute need of our times is to learn to LIVE THEURGICALLY. This is defined as "to LIVE AS RESPONSIBLE HUMAN BEINGS . . . to LIVE and ENFLESH the objectives and possibilities contained in the RITUALS we use!" In other words, to live Magically.

About the Author

PETER ROCHE de COPPENS was born May 24, 1938 in Vevey, Switzerland, and was educated in Switzerland, Argentina and Italy through secondary school, and in the United States, Germany and Canada at the University level. He graduated with honors from Columbia University, Phi Beta Kappa. Recipient of two Woodrow Wilson grants and received his Ph.D. from Fordham University in Sociology in 1972. In 1978, he received an MSW from the University of Montreal with a specialization in humanistic psychotherapy. He has studied with Pitirim Sorokin of Harvard University and was trained in Psychosynthesis by Roberto Assagioli of Florence, Italy.

He practices psychotherapy using personal and transpersonal Psychosynthesis with a particular interest in existential crisis due to psychic and spiritual awakening. For the last 17 years he has been teaching at East Stroudsburg University (Pennsylvania) where he is Professor of Sociology and Anthropology.

In 1980 he was knighted "Knight Commander of Malta." He is a member of the Board of Directors of the International Institute of Integral Human Studies of Montreal, Canada, and Vice-President of the U. S. branch, and a past Field Faculty member of the Humanistic Psychology Institute of San Francisco. He is a Fellow of the American Orthopsychiatric Association, a member of the New York Academy of Sciences, and is listed in most standard directories.

A productive writer, for the last 30 years the *Leitmotif* of his life has been the study of spirituality and the investigation and development of spiritual consciousness. In these studies he has traveled widely to meet mystics, scholars, and spiritually awakened people who have provided him with "living models" for his investigations. He belongs to and holds high Offices in several esoteric and spiritual organizations, and considers this present work to embody the very best of his personal spiritual investigations and experiences.

To Write to the Author

We cannot guarantee that every letter written to the author can be answered, but all will be forwarded on to him. Both the author and the publisher appreciate hearing from readers, learning of your enjoyment and benefit from this book. Llewellyn also publishes a bi-monthly news magazine of New Age esoteric studies and some readers' questions and comments may be answered through the *New Times'* columns if permission to do so is included in your original letter. The author participates in seminars and workshops, and dates and places may be announced in *The Llewellyn New Times*. To write to the author, or to secure a few sample copies of the *New Times* write to:

Dr. Peter Roche de Coppens
c/o THE LLEWELLYN NEW TIMES
P.O. Box 64383-Dept. 676, St. Paul, MN 55164-0383, U.S.A.

Please enclose a self-addressed, stamped envelope for reply, or $1.00 to cover expenses.

About Llewellyn's Spiritual Sciences Series

SIMPLE, PRACTICAL, EFFECTIVE, COMPREHENSIVE,
AUTHORITATIVE, INDIGENOUS TO OUR CULTURE

In a world and time that is becoming more complex, challenging and stressful, filled with "over choice" and "cognitive confusion," we are making available to you a unique series of books for self-exploration and growth that have the following distinctive features:

They are designed to be simple, cutting through abstraction, complexities and nuances that confuse and diffuse rather than enlighten, and focus your understanding of your life's purpose.

They are practical; theory always leading to practice to be crowned by devotion when followed through by you as the experimenter. You are the ultimate "laboratory" and "judge."

They are effective, for if you do the work, you will obtain results of psychospiritual transformation and expansion of consciousness.

They are comprehensive because they integrate the exoteric with the esoteric, the sacred traditions of the past with the best insights of modern science.

They are authoritative because they are all written by persons who have actually lived and experienced what they tell you about.

They are part of our Western Culture and philosophical and Mystery Traditions, which must be understood if the synthesis of the Eastern and Western spiritual traditions and Universal Brotherhood is to be realized.

This series will reconcile the fragmented aspirations of ourselves, synthesize religion and science to bring about that psychosynthesis which is the greatest need of our age and its highest aspiration.

Other Books by Peter Roche de Coppens

Ideal Man in Classical Sociology,
   Pennsylvania State University Press, 1976
Spiritual Man in the Modern World,
   University Press of America, 1976
The Nature and Use of Ritual,
   University Press of America, 1977, 1979
Spiritual Perspective,
   University Press of America, 1980
*Spiritual Perspectives II: The Spiritual Dimension and
   Implications of Love, Sex, and Marriage*,
   University Press of America, 1981
The Nature and Use of Ritual for Spiritual Attainment,
   Llewellyn Publications, 1985

Forthcoming Books

Apocalypse Now

Llewellyn's Spiritual Perspectives Series

THE INVISIBLE TEMPLE

Peter Roche de Coppens

Foreword by Canon John Rossner

1987
LLEWELLYN PUBLICATIONS
St. Paul, Minnesota, 55164-0383, U.S.A.

International Standard Book Number: 0-87542-676-X
Library of Congress Catalog Number: 87-45111

First Edition, 1987
First Printing, 1987
Second Printing, 1987

Library of Congress Cataloging-in-Publication Data

Roche de Coppens, Peter.
    The invisible temple

    (Llewellyn's spiritual sciences series)
    1. Occult sciences—Religious aspects—Christianity.
    2. Ritual. 3. Spiritual life. 4. Magic. I. Title. II. Series.
BR115.03R63   1987   248   87-45111
ISBN 0-87542-676-X (pbk)

Cover Painting: Martin Cannon
Illustrations: Nancy Benson

Produced by Llewellyn Publications
Typography and Art property of Chester-Kent, Inc.

Published by
LLEWELLYN PUBLICATIONS
A Division of Chester-Kent, Inc.
P.O. Box 64383
St. Paul, MN 55164-0383, U.S.A.

Printed in the United States of America

Dedication

This work is dedicated to all those men and women who are working with, or will be working with, the Circle of Light Generator to better themselves, help others and make this world a better place.

May the Light bless us and unite us all.

ACKNOWLEDGEMENTS:

I wish to thank Richard Urich for his patient and hard work in editing and illustrating the manuscript of this book, Carl Llewellyn Weschcke and his staff for publishing it, and the countless students and friends who have motivated its creation.

NOTE: Throughout this book, I have used the words "Man" and "Candidate" to mean, of course, both men and women. For the sake of brevity, I have used the pronouns "his" and "him," implying also "her." In selected places, I have also used the form "he/she" and "him/her" to anchor and emphasize the former.

In dealing with the "Divine Spark," the "Lord," the "Holy Spirit" and various manifestations of the Divine, I have used the pronouns "He/Him" and "It/Its" implying also "She/Her." This I have done fully recognizing that the Divine Essence, or God, is Androgynous, above and implying all genders, masculine and feminine, personal and transpersonal, singular and plural.

CONTENTS

FOREWORD

The Invisible Temple
in Historical Perspective

In *The Invisible Temple* Peter Roche de Coppens has presented us with a rich storehouse of esoteric insight into the
nature and uses of ritual, theurgy, and the High Magick of
sacramental action in a specifically Christian form and context.

Dr. Roche de Coppens — a professor of sociology at
East Stroudsburg University in Pennsylvania — has used
his skills as a writer, his familiarity with Jungian and Transpersonal psychologies, and his knowledge of Eastern esoteric tradition to produce a delightful system of Christian
"magical exercises."

In this work he displays an appreciation of the central
psychic and spiritual transformations that true religion and
ritual are meant to bring about. He presents a much needed
expose of a forgotten Christian form of the ancient esoteric
sciences and technologies of the psyche and spirit which
were intended to bring down the Divine Energies from
Heaven to Earth.

Like The Magician in the Tarot deck, or the Renaissance Alchemist in his laboratory, the seeker's high priestly
function is to create the conditions, design the channels,
and build an "Invisible Temple" into which the Power, the

Divine Life might flow. That "Invisible Temple" is our own body-and-soul instrument, and ultimately, the whole Planet Earth itself.

That is, of course, the foundational premise for all Magical Work in the highest sense, as well as that of the original fully Orthodox and Catholic "Incarnational theology" of the Christian Religion in its earliest form. In that often misunderstood great Magickal Invocation known as the Lord's Prayer, Jesus is depicted by the writers of the canonical Gospels as praying: "Thy Kingdom come, Thy Will be done, in the Earth Plane, as It already is in the Heavenly Places." This prayer, in fact, rests upon an occult conception which was widespread in the ancient world both before and after the advent of the Christian religion. In the tradition of Alexandrian Hermetic magic of the early Christian era, "Power From Heaven" invoked by the "Divine magician" or theurgist could transform the hearts of human beings and restore the Earth "After the Image of the Higher Spheres" as "Its Heavenly Prototype."

This contrasts markedly with the various world-denying varieties of Gnosticism in which the majority of human beings and the world itself were considered beyond redemption, and where the only recourse for the Gnostic was to escape entirely into the higher realms. For Christians and Hermeticists alike, the fallen world could be redeemed through the Divine Work in which the proclamation of its Message and the practice of theurgy or sacramentalism played central roles.

It is not important that academics and theologians find explicit historical or dogmatic sanction from modern versions of established Christian traditions for the specific, imaginative interpretations of the classical Christian prayers, ascriptions, and ritual actions which Peter Roche de Coppens treats. For he transcends all such exercises by appealing to Hermeticism's more ancient and universal esoteric precedents rooted in archetypes of the primordial religion, myth, and magic of the human soul. Jesus, Paul and the other Founders of Christianity, after all, did the same in their day.

It was this Primordial Tradition of archetypical intuition and insight upon which some of the earliest Pre-Nicean Fathers of the church (e.g. Lactantius, Clement, Origen, et al.) themselves also sought to build the new Christian Faith in their day. The fact that it has been forgotten and frequently abused by religious, scientific, and political establishments in the subsequent history of Western civilization does not in the least detract from its reality, efficacy, or power over us.

Readers of this book will be rewarded with the rediscovery of such arcane truths. But, as might be expected, *readers* will not get as much out of it as *practitioners* of its contents will gain for the expansion of their minds and the growth of their souls. For this book is a manual of powerful spiritual exercises and psychological techniques *that work.*

The ancient knowledge (gnosis) of metaphysical realities, and the psychic and spiritual skills that allow the human soul (psyche) to navigate inner spaces and parallel dimensions of this and other universes are forgotten truths in our world.

In modern Western Culture we tend to restrict our very ideas of science and technology to physical things alone, like building bridges, rockets, or computers. But in the ancient world in which Christianity was born, there were non-physical technologies, or technologies of the mind and spirit by which—it was believed—objective things could be accomplished in the real world.

Foremost among such non-physical or psychic and spiritual technologies was ritual magic, or the use of enacted symbolic visualizations in psychodramas produced in order to portray and set in motion various intentions and energies. When released, amplified, and assisted by various non-physical forces or entities, such human intentions and energies could—it was said—"move mountains."

It is this kind of "ritual magic" that Peter Roche de Coppens would have us learn, once again, and to practice. His predecessors in this regard include such Renaissance *Magi* as Ficino, Pico della Mirandola, Girodano Bruno, and Dr. John Dee, all of whom advocated and practiced Christian forms of ritual magic. All of these luminaries were either frowned upon, or like Bruno, martyred by the very Church that they sought to revive with their primordial insights. Nevertheless, the Church has matured somewhat since then, in tolerance if not in esoteric insight, concerning its own spiritual and psychic origins. We can reasonably expect, therefore, that this book may now contribute to the cause of enlightenment in contemporary Christian as well as secular circles.

The highest form of ritual magic involved the invocation of the gods, various angelic hierarchies, or Divinity as the underlying substratum of all things in the world. This highest form of magic—as systematized by the temple priesthood of ancient Persia—was known as *mageia,* and the priests who performed it were called "magi." In Egypt during the Hellenistic period from c. 330 B.C. to the Christian era this "high magic"was known as theurgia, or theurgy. Theurgy literally comes from two Greek words, *Theos,* or God, and *urgos,* or work. Thus theurgy was the work of God, or the Divine activity in which man participated through his knowledge of metaphysical principles which governed the universe and his skill in applying psychic rituals. Thus, Genesis depicts man as a "co-creator together with God." Man's task it is to " . . . till and keep the Garden."

Those who could participate in this Divine work were known in many of the ancient sacral cultures as the "Wise Ones"; their Divine knowledge was a "Gnosis" which led to

"Wisdom." Thus we read in the book of Exodus that Moses, as a prince of Egypt, " . . . was learned in all of the Wisdom of Egypt," meaning its Theurgy, or Divine Magic, the cumulative psychic and spiritual skills of the ancient world.

For the reader's information, I should say that such high ritual magic or theurgy was an essential and central element in all of the great religious traditions of the ancient world. Hellenistic Judaism and primitive Christianity were no exceptions. In its Christian form, ritual magic came to include such familar sounding mainline practices as prayer and sacrament, exorcisms, healings, participation in a sacred lustration, or washing ceremony, as part of an initiation into the Mysteries of Redemption, and partaking of a sacred meal, or Holy Communion, in which the Body and Blood of the Primal Man (i.e. God) were consumed by the faithful under the symbolic types of bread and wine.

This ritualized form of psychic and spiritual identification of the worshipper with God—through the central cult figure, or God-man—depended upon an earlier widespread pagan comprehension of ritual magic in Egyptian, Persian, and Graeco-Roman Mystery Rites. It was first incorporated into Hellenistic Jewish circles, and then into Apostolic Christianity from the latter's very inception.

In Christianized forms of ritual magic—inherited from Essenes, Therapeuts and other Jewish mystical-cum-magical sects—the non-physical forces and entities of the invisible universe, which prayer and sacrament were believed to engage, included not only the Holy Spirit of God and specifically named archangels, angels, deceased saints, patriarchs and prophets, but now also the Divinized Messiah, or Christ himself—as the Christain version of the Primal Man, or God-Man—as well as Mary as the Mother of God, and countless apotheocized or divinized and ascended martyrs, apostles, and confessors of the new (but in fact very old) Faith.

The objectives expected by the practitioners of Christianized forms of ritual—magic, theurgy, or sacramentalism regularly included such miraculous boons as the healing of the sick at a distance by paranormal means, the provisions of food, clothing, housing, work or physical prosperity in general, as well as guidance in daily living, protection in the act of danger, inspiration in all manner of arts and sciences, and—most important of all—endowment with the "Gifts" and "Fruits" of the Spirit.

The "Gifts" of the Spirit included various psychic and spirit powers such as prophecy and healing of the sick; the "Fruits" of the Spirit were the great virtues of the old mystery cults and of the Hermetic corpus: love, joy, peace, forgiveness, patience, and selfless-service to others, the polar opposites of the Seven Deadly Sins. Because ritual magic or theurgy—whether in its pagan or Christian form—was believed to be an effective technology of the body, mind, and spirit for obtaining such heavenly blessings, it was an essential part of religion.

In ancient sacral cultures religion itself was universally believed to be a true science, in fact the highest form of science upon which the whole schema or Divine Plan for personal transformation and human psychospiritual evolution depended. Religion—in the generic sense of the term—was the applied science of the human psyche and spirit, the function of which was to integrate the whole person—in body, mind, and spirit—with the Deity or with the authentic "Ground of Being," however that might be conceived.

This fact is very much more obvious in the Latin language where the word *religio* (from the verb *religo, religare*) has the root meaning of "to bind together," or "to integrate." Thus, surprising though it may be to some—religion and yoga essentially denoted the same thing. Both words, the one in Latin, the other in Sanskrit—designated systems of physical, mental, and spiritual practice scientifically designed for the achievement of Self-Integration, At-One-Ment with an Immanent and/or Transcendant Divinity and hence God-Realization.

In the widest sense, therefore, religion included ritual magic and theurgy, just as the apostolic Christian Faith came to incorporate prayer and sacrament as essential elements in a comprehensive "science" of psyche and spirit.

In a Primordial Tradition of higher intuition and esoteric insight, which was widespread in various esoteric groups in many ancient lands after the conquests of Alexander the Great, the whole process of human spiritual evolution and growth looked forward ultimately to the production of a New Race of human beings. Ritual magic, theurgy, the mysteries, liturgies, sacraments, and sacramental rites were among the instruments by which such human transformations were to be brought about by God-inspired souls working under the aegis of various saints, masters, and apotheocized god-men. All of this was the background against which various Hellenized Jewish mystical sects expected the coming of a Messiah and a Messianic Age.

Descriptions of such a process of human transformations may be found in the various technical terms, ciphers, and code words employed in the sacred scriptures of man in the world's religions: "Justification, Salvation, Sanctification" (Christianity); "Self-Realization" (Hinduism); "Liberation" (Buddhism) etc. The one common denominator in most of the world's great religions (at least the ones whose appeal has survived throughout the ages) is the explicit or implicit message that ordinary people—who often behave in sub-human ways half of the time—can indeed be transformed or changed into something better, something more fully human and hence more Divine, God-like, or at least more Authentic, and less distorted.

The highest goal of religion—and of its faithful servant ritual magic or prayer and sacrament—was therefore, ultimately, *the attainment of the highest states of consciousness and being.* For mystics or initiates of all traditions the experience of such Transcendental states was beyond all conceptualization. But real transformations—including those in human values and ethical sensitivities—frequently accompanied the achievement of such higher states of being and consciousness in the most successful of religion's practitioners, i.e. in the saints and the masters.

Although the latter have been few in the history of an otherwise still primitive humanity, these great exceptional souls—the saints and masters—have often been recognized—it is said—by those who have "the eyes to see and the ears to hear," as the Pioneers or First—Fruits of a New Creation, i.e., examples of a new species of humanity ahead of their time.

It is for the inauguration of such a New Creation, and a New Humanity in a New Age, " . . . in the Christ," that Peter Roche de Coppens has provided us with this book. I am happy to be able to recommend it to you for use in the building of your very own "Invisible Temple."

John Rossner
Department of Religion
Concordia University, &
International Institute
of Integral Human Sciences
Montreal
February 5th, 1987

1
INTRODUCTION

*Practical Guidelines for the Operation of a
Personal and Group Consciousness Transformer*

Since the publication of *The Nature and Use of Ritual for
Spiritual Attainment,* little time has gone by but much has
happened. I have received many letters from readers
commenting on their understanding and personal experiences with the materials and psychospiritual exercises that
were suggested in that work, and requesting further
information and applications. The same has happened, for
a long time, with people in various groups using these
materials and techniques, and getting different results. On
my own spiritual journey, I have also gone beyond and
expanded those materials and their practical applications.
In all cases, however, the fundamental questions were
exactly the same:

> **Where do we go from here? How do we work
> with and apply this perspective, with its related
> techniques, in our daily lives?—in our personal
> growth work, with a specialized "spiritual group,"
> and in our religious life? What is the next practical
> step? What is the next and bigger stepping
> stone?**

It is questions like these, springing from all quarters

beginning with myself, extending to the members of various "Operational Groups," and culminating with the readers of *The Nature and Use of Ritual for Spiritual Attainment* that have given birth to the present work, *The Invisible Temple*. This work is thus an organic sequence to the previous book, as well as a practical book that can be used independently by interested and committed men and women of good will who have come to the conclusion that the Great Work is the most important work of our times. For this is, indeed, the fundamental Challenge of Our Times, what history seems to be demanding of us at this crucial juncture, not only for our personal and collective psychospiritual survival but also, and especially, for taking the next qualitative step in our evolution—**For becoming more than what we are and what we are truly meant to be as full human beings. For becoming adult human beings, the sons and daughters of our Mother Earth and of our Father Sky.**

Who is this book for? I envisage the following types of persons:

- First and foremost for you who have read *The Nature and Use of Ritual* and who want to further develop, explore, and embody the perspective, techniques, and possibilities outlined therein.
- For Christians who are interested in the mystical and "living" aspect of their religion and who are serious about consciously working towards bringing about the Second Coming of Christ in their own *heart, soul, and being.*
- For students of the Occult, Mystical, and Magical Traditions who are not only interested in obtaining an intellectual understanding of the nature and implications of Spiritual Initiation, but who are actively seeking to *bring it about.*
- For men and women who are training for, or actually

are, Priests and Priestesses, in various Christian and even non-Christian Traditions, and who want to put more Light and Power in their Rituals and Services, and by resonance, to awaken the same in their congregations or groups.

- For students and leaders of the Sacred Traditions who want simple, practical, and time-proven means to:

  Awaken their intuition and activate the inspirational flow from within.
  Make the symbols, images, and rituals of their tradition "speak" again to them and "come alive" in their being and lives.
  Achieve a conscious and growing communion with the divine within.

- For solitary students who do not yet have a teacher or "operational group," but who are seeking one, or for students, teachers, and groups who are interested in experimenting with and perhaps integrating with their own work the materials we are presenting.

- For theology students, students of comparative religions, and inquisitive minds who want to develop a spiritual understanding of the various Religions, Sacred Traditions, and the Mysteries.

- For all those who are wondering about the Riddle of the Sphinx, the Mystery of Life, and the Enigma of the Universe, and whether life on Earth does have a higher meaning and purpose, and if so, how they can be unveiled.

- For those who are pondering over the mastery of Evil and Suffering and what they can *personally* do about it in their lives and in the world.

The greatest and ultimate mystery as well as Miracle is, indeed, as has been pointed out by the greatest men and women of all ages, the Saints, Sages, and Heroes of all times, *life itself.* And, if *life* is *the sacred* par excellence, then indeed it behooves us to develop that Reverence for Life, that inner and inextinguishable urge towards Life, towards a *Life More Abundant.* Moreover, as we have pointed out in our previous works: Life and Light, Life and Love, Life and Power, and Life and Action are indistinguishable, being one and the same thing. How then can we *consciously* and *systematically* live in such a fashion as to *facilitate that great current of Life, Love,* and *Power* in our being and in that of others? How can we generate more *Life,* more *Fire* and more *Energy* in our being and in our daily lives? These are the vital questions we shall tackle in the present work, and for the realization of which I will suggest simple, practical, effective, and time-proven ways. For this after all is what the Great Work is all about—*to become more alive, more oneself, and to better express that self!*

To accomplish the foregoing and to include in this work a *most important tool* designed to dynamize, intensify, and amplify the work that is done individually by the Candidate or by his Group, Temple, or Church, we have introduced what I have called "an Energy, Consciousness, and Light Generator, Transformer, and Amplifier" which will be described and analyzed in detail in a later chapter. This is what used to be called the "Magical Circle," the "Circle of Light" or the "Power Chain" by various Traditions, both solar (spiritually oriented) and lunar (psychically oriented).

This tool can add immeasurably to the personal work of Concentration, Meditation, Contemplation, and Theurgy by introducing Group Work in the process of *Psychospiritual Transformation,* both as actual Group Work, Visualized Group Work, and as Inner Plane Group Work. To better grasp the nature and function of this tool, let me remind you that the very quintessence of genuine spiritual work involves *Upaya* (the practice of spiritual exercises) and *Satsang* (Group Work) in the Buddhist Tradition, and the *worship of God* and *the building of His Church* in the Western Tradition—which amounts to the same thing. That Jesus Himself stated "Where two or three of you shall be assembled in my name, there I shall be in the midst of them." And that one of the core teachings of modern Sociology is that *human interaction brings about a creative Psychic Synthesis.*

This is not to say that the Candidate must wait to have an "operational group" to begin working in earnest, either with the materials presented in this work or with other materials, but simply that he or she should be aware of this important tool and of its different uses. At some point along the Path, it should not prove too difficult for the Candidate, either alone, with a teacher, or with a group of like-minded friends to set up such a "Generator." For just as "when the student is ready, the teacher appears" so also when the time is ripe for Group Work, the right persons will appear and a group will be easily put together! Moreover, there are phases of this Circle of Light Generator which can also be lived through without an actual group on the physical Plane.

I have personally experimented with all the phases of the operation of such a Generator (as described in this work) and found it very easy to gather together such an "experimental group" in whatever city or country I have found myself for a certain period of time. The setting up of such a group can be challenging, *fun*, and the natural thing to do at a certain point in one's study, growth, and training with many spiritual, psychological, and mundane benefits accruing from it.

In the formulation of his "Islamic Revolution" Khomeni stated a very profound and fundamental truth that answers a basic urge of the human Spirit and a vital demand of the "Spirit of our Times." Unfortunately, as it often happens in human affairs, he misunderstood it and misapplied it for selfish and political personality ends. This truth is:

> God has created us and a Spark of God has been infused in the deepest and highest recesses of our being. The everpresent and everlasting *yearning* of that Spark is that, consciously or unconsciously, we might *connect ourselves with God*, the Whole. It is this yearning and striving to reconnect ourselves consciously with Him who has brought us into being which enables the revolutionaries of the Islamic Republic to move forward and not to fear, or to back down before any danger. God is Great and we are his Martyrs.

Our present human and spiritual challenge, as I understand it, is precisely to redefine and reapply, in a loving, constructive, and creative fashion, this basic yearning and striving of our being to achieve the great goal of having the *whole world becoming the true home for all human beings*. Or rather the "crucible," "Laboratory," or "school" wherein all human beings can consciously work at perfecting themselves and each other to find the *Right Relationship* with each other, with Life, and thus with the *Whole*.

The overall perspective and tradition we have chosen for our work is that of Christianity, with its Body (Symbols, Images, Prayers, and Rituals) and Spirit (The Light, Power, and Life that stand behind the Symbols, Images, Prayers, and Rituals). This for two reasons: First, because as St. Augustine pointed out, Christianity is not a New Religion but the *Living Synthesis* of the Wisdom of the Sacred Traditions, and hence, of all Religions, expressed in simple, practical, and effective terms for our Age. Second, because in the West most people are born at least "nominal Christians," and because there are many Christian Traditions, churches, and services that are functioning wherever one might find oneself but without a *Spiritual explanation of what they are doing* and how Worship could be carried out in the light of both the ancient mystical Teachings and the latest developments of the modern natural and social sciences. A New Age is slowly dawning upon us which we are all, consciously or unconsciously, bringing about, and this New Age requires of us *a new soul* or *explanation* of our religious and spiritual lives.

The Esoteric Tradition we have chosen to give birth to that new soul or spiritual explanation is that of the *Qabalah*. This again for two basic reasons: First, because the Christian Symbols, Images, Prayers, and Rituals were actually drawn from a Qabalistic Tradition which can best explain and activate their *Mysteries* (The Mysteries of Jesus). My fundamental assumption here is that the Teachers and Fathers who developed Christianity were well-acquainted with and drawing from the Qabalah, both Jewish and Universal. Second, because the Qabalah, based on the Tree of Life with its Spheres and their connecting Paths, IS our own indigenous Western Esoteric Tradition which is most suitable for our contemporary way of life. Another and final reason might be because the Qabalah, more than any other system I am acquainted with, can function as an *open system* by which to correlate, interpret, and synthesize all Spiritual Traditions, Eastern, Western, or Primitive, with the contemporary developments of modern Science.

This means that our readers and Candidates should become well-acquainted with the Qabalistic Tradition. They can do this by reading the volumes of the Llewellyn Spiritual Sciences Series as well as other Llewellyn publications, the works of Dion Fortune, Israel Regardie, and of Melita Denning and Osborne Phillips in particular, and other excellent works which are now in print.

For a person new to the Qabalistic Tradition or even a student of it, the basic question obviously is: "What is the

Qabalah?" To answer this question, I would suggest turning to the well-acknowledged writers of this essential Tradition. For example, Dion Fortune defines the Qabalah as "An attempt to reduce to diagrammatic form every force and factor in the manifested *universe* and the *soul of man;* to correlate them one to another and reveal them spread out as a map so that the relative positions between them can be seen and the relations between them traced . . . a compendium of science, psychology, philosophy, and theology." Her student, W.E. Butler, writes: "The Qabalah is a method of using the mind in a practical and constantly widening consideration of the Universal soul of man." William Gray calls it: "Symbolic representations of the relationship believed to exist between the most abstract divinity and the most concrete humanity." And: "A family tree linking God and man with angels and other beings as a complete conscious creation." Israel Regardie suggests: "The Qabalah is a trustworthy guide, leading to a comprehension both of the Universe and of one's own Self." Alta LaDage sees it as "A system for obtaining direct religious experience." Melita Denning and Osborne Phillips explain: "In the glyph of the Tree of Life, each Sephira represents one of the archetypal spiritual states, existent not only cosmically but in the depths of each person's own being. Each Path with its attributed influence represents the *changes of consciousness* by which a specific one of those states can be attained from one or the other of the Sephiroth which are placed lower on the Tree of Life. Knowledge and practice in achieving these controlled changes is thus a most potent means of spiritual progress, of inner initiation, and of establishing an effective relationship with the deeper levels of one's psyche."

Finally, Ellen Cannon Reed in her excellent book, *The Witches' Qabala* (Llewellyn Publications, 1985) looks at the Qabalah as:

> Providing a filing cabinet for the mind, giving you a

place for everything. Even better, the Qabala offers a retrieval system, not only for information *you* have placed in this cabinet, but eventually for information placed there over the centuries by other practitioners of Qabalism. The Qabala is a way of tying all your studies together, relating them to each other, enabling you to understand each more completely. It is also a tool that can be used to guide your personal growth, and to measure it. It can be used for personal and for group work, by solitary, student and teacher . . . Legend has it that the Qabala was given to ancient Hebrew scholars by an archangel for the purpose of helping them experience the Mysteries, and to help others experience them . . . It is valid. It works, that is what is truly important, and it works today in our world, in our culture, our way of life, our religion. It is a *living* system, a growing one, ancient and ever new.

I would view the Qabalah as all of the foregoing and much more! For our present purposes, however, I would say that the Qabalah is the underlying Fountain and Groundwork upon which all of the Rituals and Documents outlined and discussed in this work are rooted, and which is thus indispensable in order to give birth to a new Soul, to a modern and practical explanation of them, and especially, to live them theurgically!

One of the most important and pressing demands of our times, what history seems to be demanding of us now, is to learn how to *live theurgically.* What does this really mean? It means, essentially, to learn how to progressively *Live* and *Incarnate* our ideals, to "make the Word become flesh" or to become the "Artists" and "Co-Creators" of our being and destiny—to *live responsibly as human beings.* It means, in other words, to *live* and *enflesh* the objectives and possibilities contained in the *rituals* we use!

Edgar Mitchell, the Apollo 14 Astronaut, when he founded his Institute of Noetic Sciences, stated:

There are no unnatural or supernatural phenomena, only large gaps in our knowledge of what is natural . . .

We should strive to fill those gaps of ignorance.

This is precisely the central objective of the Llewellyn Spiritual Sciences Series at the cognitive-philosophical level, and of this particular work at the practical-experiential level.

To achieve this great goal we have sought to reconcile and integrate the very best insights and training of the Sacred Traditions of the past with the latest developments and paradigms of the modern natural and social sciences. This should lead, by degrees and in various individual ways, to the unfoldment of an open and growing Philosophy of Life and a practical Art of Living. Within this larger and more comprehensive framework I feel that the specific aim of this book is to personalize, make operational, and enflesh the core teachings of *The Nature and Use of Ritual for Spiritual Attainment.* Here *you* the reader can take *yourself,* your own Field of Consciousness and Aura, and a group of like-minded men and women who share the same high ideals, and who are willing not only to *meditate upon* and *discuss* the Great Work but to *do it* and *live it* as the *essential laboratory* to test and refine the basic insights, exercises, and teachings suggested by the above-mentioned work.

What was proposed as a set of guidelines and as a "Path-map" by the author must now be followed and explored by You, the reader, in your own consciousness and daily life to be redefined, personalized, rendered "alive" and incarnated in your own unique way and being. For this kind of work and achievement must be tested and retested by *each person* and *each generation* to be truly authentic and living. The really *esoteric* spiritual Mysteries and Teachings can only be discovered and mastered by *direct personal experience, work, and living.* There simply is no other way!

The great Symbols, Rituals, and Exercises of the Spiritual Tradition can only unveil their Mysteries and guide the Candidate to the Great Work by *themselves from within his or her own consciousness and experience.* All the rest, useful as it may be, remains an external, intellectual philosophy and set of possibilities and not a *Living Reality.*

Before beginning with the actual practical work, there are three very important points I wish to make that you, the reader and Candidate, should ever bear in mind and meditate upon throughout your experiments and work with the materials presented in this book. These are:

1. As the Yoga Sutras of Pantanjali pointed out thousands of years ago, as Jesus of Nazareth never ceased to admonish and emphasize, and as every great and authentic spiritual teacher has always taught:

    "The great work of personal transformation, of the expansion of human consciousness, and the attainment of spiritual consciousness *must* be grounded in a moral, balanced, and healthy life, called "Living the Life" or simply "Holiness," and not in various Yoga or Esoteric exercises and techniques.

    If you are not willing or ready to change your life, your relationships, and your very *self, do not* enter this Path or practice the suggested exercises as they will either not work or lead to drastic consequences which could be very costly and painful to you and those you are associated with.

    This is the truly essential precondition to do this work effectively and the parting of the way between those who would really transform themselves and their lives, *no matter what the cost,* and those who would acquire the expertise and techniques to satisfy the desires of their personality, to feed their human ego, and force change upon the world and others.

This has been said many times in many ways, but it is so fundamental that we must state it clearly and explicitly, once again, at the beginning of this work. For this work, as all true spiritual work, leads to the fullest development of one's personality, the actualization of all of one's faculties, and the refining and strengthening of one's will . . . only to surrender them to God (the Higher Self), once this preparatory work has been accomplished, and not for their own sake . . . as the contemporary American Gospel of Success and Prosperity seems to indicate!

The final and truest "reward" of this Great Work will not be health, wealth, the finding of a suitable mate, or worldly success . . . (which, at best, could only be a by-product) but, instead, to *know the true living God, one's very Higher Self, and to do His will on Earth, to work for His own inscrutable plans and purpose.*

2. The Energy, Consciousness, and Light Generator, Transformer, and Amplifier can be established and used in two basic ways and on two different dimensions which can be synchronized with each other:

   A. The horizontal, *external*, physical dimension, which consists of forming a Circle of Light with a select group of like-minded men and women of good will and then doing this work in a group setting.

   B. The vertical, *internal*, psychological dimension which consists of forming the Circle of Light within one's own Aura with the various Psychospiritual Centers and then doing this work *alone* within one's own Temple and Sanctuary.

Much later, when one has mastered both the inner and the outer Laboratory or Theater, one can then proceed to form the outer Circle of Light linking and integrating both the vertical and the horizontal dimensions *in one's imagination.* This is done by invoking the regular participants and *visualizing* them at their usual place in the Circle, calling their names and feeling and experiencing the Light-Energy flow being activated in the Circle of Light. Finally, the same operation can also be performed (by the experienced and advanced Candidate) *on the Inner Planes,* in an out-of-the-body state, in the Greater Inner Plane Sanctuary . . . But of course, those who have reached this stage will have become spiritually autonomous and "guided from within," and will thus no longer need external teachers or books such as the present one!

3. While it is very useful to have a Teacher or Guide on the Physical Plane and to have Companions on the Path, this is not always possible, nor is it indispensable, as there may be many different parts of the Path, at the beginning, in the middle, and in the end, when one will find oneself (seemingly) *alone,* and will have to walk alone . . .

This book is intended to be of help precisely to those aspirants and candidates who do not have a genuine guide, and who may have to begin alone, without a group *in the Physical World* . . . which they may, themselves, constitute at a later stage on the path.

In such case, it is very important to bear four things in mind:

- That *Discipline* and *Regular Practice* are a must! This work must be done again and again, even if no immediate or apparent results occur for a relatively long period of time. Eventually, and in their own time (in the "time of the Higher Self") they will inevitably and unfailingly occur, many times imperceptibly at first.
- A *Diary* and *Workbook* must be religiously kept. The diary describing and analyzing the unfoldment of one's general daily life and events, the workbook describing what exercises or work are being done, where, when, and under what conditions, and with what immediate and tangible results and consequences.
- It is recommended that the Consciousness Checklist (see Appendix C) be used before beginning the actual work, during the work, and at the end of the work to develop Inner Observation and to monitor what is really happening in the Inner Theater or Laboratory of one's consciousness. This is very important and often overlooked or neglected because of the time involved, but what an opportunity it becomes to develop self-knowledge and train the Will!
- A Special Place should also be set aside and consecrated for the Great Work. This could range all the way from setting up a special room in one's house as one's *Personal Temple* which must only be entered into for the

work and then only by the people who are participating in the work. This in order to build up and feed an appropriate specialized "psychic atmosphere" or Egregor (much as the old homes had a Chapel in them) . . . to sitting in a special chair or in a special plane in one's bed to the same work with the construction of an Altar and Sanctuary, to a special place in one's room, acting as the middle ground between the two extremes.

Now as to the specifics of how this book is to be used. Each part or chapter of this work entails the *Use* and *Further Training of* entering into, utilizing, and developing:

The Aura or Alembic*, the Inner Consciousness of the Candidate: learning to visualize and experience one's own Aura as a *Light, Energy,* and *Consciousness Field* extending, like an egg, about 10–20 inches from one's physical body radiating various and changing colors, frequencies, and vibrations (see Illustration of the Human Aura).

2. **The Tree of Life:** learning to visualize, formulate, and experience one's Tree of Life with its various Spheres or *Psychospiritual Centers* in their correct locations, colors, and vibrations (see Appendix B).

3. **The "Core Muscles of Consciousness,"** the basic Tools of the Candidate: learning to know and work effectively with the seven *functions of the psyche* and their related Psychospiritual Processes:

---

*ALEMBIC: This word was used by the Alchemists to denote the Energy Field around a human being, known today as the AURA.

Willing and the ability
    to Concentrate
Thinking and the ability
    to Meditate
Feeling and the ability to
    express Devotion
Imagination and the ability
    to Visualize
Intuition and the ability to
    activate Invocation/Evocation

These are the "Core Muscles of Consciousness"

Biopsychic Drives (Desires and
    Impulses) and the ability to
    Transform and Direct Energy
Sensation and the ability to use
    inner and outer Observation

4. **The Four Fundamental Stages of Personal Transformation, Consciousness Expansion, and Spiritual Awakening:** learning how to progressively move through:

CONCENTRATION: directing all of one's attention upon the work at hand to the exclusion of everything else.

MEDITATION: directing all of one's thoughts and knowledge upon the work at hand, seeking to grasp cognitively and fully what one is doing.

CONTEMPLATION: having altered one's state of consciousness, becoming AT ONE with what one is doing: becoming the symbol or the Ritual itself . . .

THEURGY: creating an inner reality into which one will live and experience the work one is doing, and then progressively incarnate or become this Reality in one's daily life, which will be shaped and constructed *from within* rather than emerging and being constructed from without by external stimuli.

By way of conclusion, let the aspiring Candidate always keep present in his or her consciousness that the WORK must first be KNOWN BY THE HEAD, then FELT BY THE HEART, then CHOSEN BY THE WILL, to be LIVED BY THE BODY, SO THAT ONE CAN MAKE THE "WORD BECOME FLESH" OR *BECOME* THE IDEAL ONE IS NURTURING.

2
LIGHT AND ENERGY GENERATOR

The Development and Operation of an Energy,
Consciousness, and Light Generator,
Transformer, and Amplifier

If all the multifarious and contradictory yearnings and strivings of human beings were to be summarized into one essential striving it would be:

> **For a life more abundant,**
> **For becoming more alive, vivifying the various**
> **aspects and expressions of their being,**
> **For consciously knowing and perfecting them-**
> **selves!**

Specifically, I would argue that, in seeking to become more Alive, a human being is really attempting to expand his consciousness in order to *know more,* to quicken his heart or feel more deeply and passionately, to *love more,* and to dynamize his self-expression or *intensify his will* and his *creative energies.*

This is truly the most universal and perennial drive to

which all human beings give conscious or unconscious expression. It is here that the Spiritual Traditions of both East and West, and this workbook in particular, have truly substantial contributions to make. The central thesis of this work is simply that: it is possible for *any man or woman of good will*, who is deeply and genuinely interested in *living more consciously and fully*, in becoming more alive, and in enabling others to achieve the same goal, *to deliberately work towards this great end* by creating what I have called an "Energy, Consciousness, and Light Generator, Transformer, and Amplifier."

All that is required here is to *use one's own consciousness and being* and one's *chosen group* (if one is available) *as the actual laboratory wherein to carry out experiments that will demonstrate and incarnate the principles and truths that are suggested.* Specifically, what is required is:

1. Knowledge and understanding of the basic theory, principles, and techniques that are involved.

2. A small group of like-minded men and women of good will who are committed to the Great Work, comprising ideally between 7 and 14 people (or, for those who are working alone until such a group can be organized, the visualization of the aura with the Tree of Life activated and the circulation of light and power between the 10 Psychospiritual Centers) who are willing and able to meet and work with this Generator *diligently* and *regularly*.

   Meetings and Operations for a group should take place at least once a week, while personal work should be done once a day for a minimum of 5–9 months.

3. The true *mysteries* and *power* of this Generator can only be discovered and experienced in one way: *by using it!* By doing this work regularly and

diligently over a long period of time, with the same people or in the same way (if one does it alone). For these mysteries and powers cannot possibly be described and comprehended *intellectually,* they can only be *experienced* and *lived.* And it is the Generator *itself* that will gradually unfold and unveil its true esoteric and living nature and implications/applications. Thus it is *we,* ourselves, our Aura and Tree of Life, and *our group* (if we have one) which will crystallize and become truly alive, as well as the place or Temple in which this Generator is set up, which will become the *living laboratory and crucible whence our observations, findings, and conclusions must be drawn.*

4. Besides effective Knowledge, the right group of people and/or our Tree of Life, and plenty of good will and hard work, there is one last indispensable ingredient: consecrating one's heart or devotion to do this work! For unless one can really "open one's Heart" and pour forth one's *love* into this work, it will not become "alive" and truly "work"; instead it will remain silent and cold and whoever looks at it in this fashion will have to conclude that it does not work and is mere fantasy or wishful thinking.

    As this Generator is very closely related to our consciousness, operating as a *function of our level of consciousness,* in fact, as the very *laboratory for the transformation of our consciousness,* it very much depends upon what *we put into it,* what attitudes we have towards it, or what is generally called *Faith.* For Faith is, indeed, as all Spiritual Traditions and Religions have pointed out from time immemorial, *the Key to make any ritual or Consciousness-Transformation come "alive."*

And the essence of Faith is, like most essential things, a *Trinity,* the *Trinity of the Head, the Heart, and the Will,* or in plain English, *focusing all of our attention, thoughts,* and *feelings.* This may sound like we are belaboring a small point but it is an all-important one!

To better understand the nature and functioning of the Circle of Light Generator we are proposing to you, let us for a moment turn to the contemporary cultural scene. In both the natural and the social sciences something very interesting happened in the 20th Century: it was discovered that the observer, or the person who was carrying out an experiment, had a major impact on the results of the experiment itself and could thus be seen as an intervening variable. In Nuclear Physics this is called Heisenberg's Second Principle of Indeterminacy, whereas in Sociology it is called The Hawthorne Effect. The net implication of this is that *different subjects get different results in the same experimental situation.* This intervening variable seems to be very closely linked with the *level of consciousness* and the *level of being,* or the *vibrations and energies,* of the person carrying out the experiment . . . which now scientifically corroborates a very old teaching of the Spiritual Tradition: *that the Key to Spiritual Awakening and Understanding is to be found in the expansion of one's consciousness and in Personal Transformation.*

As the central Axiom of the Hermetic Tradition is: "As Above, so Below," we can now use this analogical principle to better visualize and grasp the basic nature and dynamics of the Circle of Light Generator we are suggesting. Let us look at an electrical generator and observe it.

The fundamental principle of the electrical generator is very simple: physical electricity (electro-motive force) is generated by a spinning core of electrical wires through a magnetic field in a rotary fashion. Our own Energy,

Consciousness, and Light Generator functions in exactly the same way, but on another plane of being and with different energies. Instead of *physical electricity,* here we are dealing with *psychic and spiritual energies*— specifically with the *Etheric* (or Vital), the *Astral* (or Emotional), the *Mental,* and the *Spiritual Energies* which are being circulated, balanced and recharged. Instead of a core of electrical wires that is spun through a magnetic field to generate a flow of electrons, here we circulate visualized and experienced light, warmth, and vibrations drawn from our own Tree of Life, or Psychospiritual Centers, into and through the Tree of Life of the different Persons in our Generator (or the Spheres of our own Tree of Life if working alone) who prismate the Light and Energy in different ways, depending on their own:

A. Level of Consciousness and Being,
B. *Faith* at the moment,
C. And ability to work in a coordinated fashion with certain "muscles of Consciousness" (to be discussed later on).

The Energy, Consciousness, and Light Generator we are suggesting to you includes four distinct phases or steps, each of which can be subdivided into a Male and a Female aspect, the aim of which is to *balance* and *recharge* a certain part of our being and consciousness. Moreover, the proper operation of the Generator itself includes two distinct phases which are well recognized in the Sacred Traditions. These are:

1. *The Preparatory or Opening Phase* and
2. *The True Work or THEURGY.*

The Preparatory or Opening Phase of the Generator contains four steps dealing with the Four Elements, and involves the proper warming-up, tuning-in, balancing, and recharging of our Etheric, Astral, Mental, and Spiritual Energies and

Vehicles of consciousness. Whereas the True Work itself and the manifold uses of the Generator include: a Female Aspect, called Entering the Silence, which involves the gradual attunement and sharpening up of our sensitivity and receptivity, and a Male Aspect, called Theurgy or Ritual, which involves the bringing down of the Divine Light, the Divine Fire, and *the Divine Creative Energies* through the use of Archetypes and Symbols operating as "Consciousness Transformers."

The Preparatory or Opening Phase of this Generator consists of the following steps, each of which must be performed in a precise order:

1. Each person in the Generator will sit in a comfortable position, making sure that there are no tensions or pains in the body.

2. After the Circle has been formed and each person is seated, the participants will hold hands and close their eyes (the sitting arrangements can be either that of the Psychic Traditions: Man-Woman, Man-Woman, or that of the Spiritual Traditions where it does not matter whether we have a Man next to a Woman or to another Man as each person is androgynous and the proper Polarity will be set up anyway!).

3. Participants will then *individually* and *collectively* make an effort of Introversion; that is, withdrawing one's attention and psychic energies from the outer/physical world to refocus them on the inner/psychic world in one's Field of Consciousness.

    Then, each person should deliberately let go of the past and of the future, and of one's fears and anxieties as well as of one's desires and aspirations to be fully *present* in the here and now.

4. At this point, the participants should direct their attention to their *hands* and begin to *experience* the

human warmth, the light, love, and energy-vibrations that naturally and spontaneously take place between themselves and the other members of the Circle of Light Generator.

They can visualize themselves as a *glass of water* (their Aura) that is slowly and gently being filled, with their hands acting as hoses, bearing in mind that they are to be giving of their excess energies and receiving of those energies that they are lacking.

This process should be continued for a certain period of time until a certain point of balance and equilibrium is established (at this point, the person in charge of the Ritual should intuitively sense when, symbolically speaking, the glass of water has been filled).

5. Then, three deep rhythmic breaths should be taken by everyone using the 7–4, 7–4 breathing count (inhale counting 7, hold counting 4, exhale counting 7, and hold counting 4 to begin the cycle anew), or any other breathing rhythm they are comfortable with, provided they inhale and exhale *deeply*. The actual intention while breathing should be to further relax the body and quicken the mind.

6. Again the attention of the participants should be directed to their hands, and they should now experience (but this time a little more consciously and intensely than before) the exchange of human warmth, or warm milk as I call it, of light, love, and life until they reach a new point of equilibrium.

7. This completes the Etheric or Vital *balancing* and *recharging* of one's energies, which is a completely *automatic* and *unconscious process,* for at this level, all that the participants can do is to hold hands to

set up the Etheric circuit, and to be *aware* and *receptive* to the energy-exchange taking place.

Having brought Peace and Life to their Etheric Body, the participants are then ready to move onto and "climb" (or "ascend") to the next level which is the Astral or Emotional level.

To move onto the next level, the Astral or Emotional level, the participants, who should still be holding hands, keeping their eyes closed (and feeling *refreshed, balanced,* and *energized* at the Etheric level) will proceed with the following steps:

1. They will now direct their attention to a point right above their physical head. There, they will visualize a radiating, pulsating *sphere of dazzling White Light,* like a noonday sun, slightly larger than their physical head, slightly above it and yet interpenetrating it, and they will try to get in touch with its Power, its Light, Warmth, and Life.

2. Next, they will visualize a ray of that Light and of those Energies slowly descending like a true Pillar of Light, moving from the Head area into the Heart area. A gentle or light pressure might be experienced along the spine as the Light and the Energies descend.

3. When the Heart area is reached by this Light and Energies it should come alive and expand like a balloon that is being blown up. One might also feel emotions being stirred-up in the Heart area.

4. A ray of the same Light and Energies should then be directed from the Heart area to the Left Shoulder area, then down along the left arm and left hand, and be circulated three times from left to right around the Circle of Light Generator.

If a person knows how to project and accompany the Light with his/her breath (exhaling/projecting the Light and Energies halfway around the Circle and then inhaling/drawing in the Light and Energies back into himself/herself for the other half of the Circle), this should be done.

Also, while circulating the Light and Energies in this fashion, each person can meditate upon the fact that he/she is moving from *Profane Space* to *Sacred Space*, with the first circling of the Light, from *Profane Time* to *Sacred Time*, with the second circling of the Light, and from *Profane Events* to *Sacred Events*, with the third circling of the Light, thereby profoundly changing his/her own consciousness and attitudes.

5. Having completed the third circling of the Light and Energies, the attention and visualization of the participants should come back to their Heart area (let us call this their Heart Center) and from there extend a ray of the same Light and Energies, and circulate them this time from *right to left*, passing through the Right Shoulder Center, the right arm and hands, and around the circle, using the same procedure as before.

6. Having now completed the third circling of the Light and Energies from right to left, the participants should now behold and contemplate the beautiful Circle of Light which exists in their midst and which links them with each other person, bringing emotional *Peace* and *Life*, or balancing and recharging their emotional energies and bodies.

They should seek to absorb and integrate as much of the present state of consciousness that they are now in, as they are capable, and to impress upon their awareness their present state of being, realizing that they can re-evoke it at will by visualizing the Circle of Light Generator.

7. The final point that participants should keep in mind at the Emotional or Astral level is that while they are forming a *horizontal circle of Light* which connects them to every other person in the Circle, they are also forming a *vertical Circle of Light* which connects their Field of Consciousness with every other Psychospiritual Center in their Tree of Life. In this fashion they are linking not only themselves to every other member of the Circle, but also their conscious mind with their Superconscious and the human self with the Spiritual Self . . . to the extent that they are individually ready for this. And now the participants are ready to move onto the next level, the Mental level.

To move onto the Mental level, the participants will use the *Namaskara Ritual,* or its functional equivalent, which can function both at the *mental* and at the *spiritual* levels, depending on their level of consciousness and being. The *Namaskara Ritual* is done as follows: participants will bow mentally to the person immediately to their left, saying inwardly:

"Namaskara, (name of the person), The Divine in me recognizes and greets the Divine in you . . ."

They might feel a slight pressure as Light and Life leave their forehead to touch the forehead of the person so greeted, and as they continue . . . "The Divine in me recognizes and greets the Divine in you . . ." they should visualize this Light and Life descending to that person's Heart Center to then return to their own Heart Center from there. They should also visualize the triple flame of a candle formulating around the person so greeted.

This procedure is then repeated for as many people as

there are in the Circle, and ideally, it should be done at least seven times (as there are seven key Psychospiritual Centers in our Tree of Life . . .)

This process should, immediately, bring *Peace* and *Life* or balance and recharge the *Mental* energies and faculties of all the members of the Circle who are, in turn, greeting others and being greeted by others.

The Circle of Light Generator can now be visualized and contemplated as being composed of all the "candle flames" of the participants (which are their activated Auras and lit Trees of Life). Once again the participants should absorb, assimilate, and integrate their present state of consciousness and energies to *purify* and *consecrate themselves* for the work to follow.

The final step of the Opening Phase is for all the participants to invoke God's Presence, Blessings, and Guidance in their own words and ways for themselves and for the group as a whole.

If properly done with enough *Faith*, by persons who are ready, this can open up the Spiritual Dimension of the participants who have just balanced and re-energized themselves on the Etheric, Astral, and Mental levels.

The Spiritual Dimension of our being and life does not need *Peace* and *Life*, or to be balanced and recharged; what it does need is to be *awakened* and *properly linked with the other three dimensions!* At the Spiritual level, the major problem is simply that we have "fallen asleep" and have cut ourselves off from the most important and essential part of our being (the true result of the "Fall"). Our basic task here is, therefore, to become aware that this dimension does in fact *exist* and to open the channels by which it can permeate our being on the three lower levels, vivifying them and integrating them properly.

The Opening or Preparatory Phase of the Generator can be used for many purposes and for preparing a sound foundation upon which to "build our Temple to the Living God" as well as to do more rewarding and advanced work. For our purposes in this work, it can be used as:

1. A "Love Vitamin Generator" capable of producing, refining, and circulating the "Love-Vitamins" which are necessary for our consciousness to function properly.

   Specifically, it can be used to systematically *relax* and *stimulate* our being and the functions of our Psyche on the Etheric, Astral, and Mental levels, and for those who are ready, also on the Spiritual level.

2. A very practical and effective way of balancing and equilibrating our various energies and drives and to dynamize and vivify our Creative Energies—something which is an indispensable prerequisite for achieving a serious and effective consciousness transformation and expansion . . . As the old Alchemists put it: "You must have Gold to produce Gold."

3. A practical laboratory and training ground to develop and coordinate the five basic "muscles of our consciousness"—*Willing* and *Concentration*, *Thinking* and *Meditation*, *Feeling* and *Devotion*, *Imagination* and *Visualization*, and finally *Intuition* and *Invocation/Evocation*.

   The Opening Phase of the Generator can also be used to systematically and regularly practice *Concentration, Meditation, Contemplation*, and *Theurgy* with appropriate Symbols, Myths, and Rituals.

4. A simple and practical way to train oneself in making any Ritual come alive and vivify the letter with the Living Spirit—an ability which can then be applied in various Church Services, Spiritual Exercises, and Personal Growth Exercises. Finally,

this ability can also be used to train oneself for partaking *consciously* of Holy Communion (the infusion of our being with the Divine Light and the Divine Fire, engendering Spiritual Life and bringing about a breakthrough of the Superconscious into the Conscious, and the eventual connection of the human self with the Spiritual Self).

5. An integrated and functional way of activating the Intuition, opening up the channels of true Inspiration leading to Illumination. This leads to the discovery and *Practical Utilization* of the Infinite Source of Wisdom and Life that lies within each human being—*the Divine Spark* Which dwells in the Superconscious and Whose Light, Fire, and Life we can progressively learn to tap and to manifest in our being and daily lives.

The Opening Phase of the Generator can be carried through with most men and women of good will without prior or specific intellectual, moral, or personal qualifications. Thus, it should be made accessible to whoever shows a true interest and is willing to invest a certain amount of attention, time, and energy to make it grow and come alive in their consciousness and being.

Nevertheless it will take a few months, roughly five to nine, before a group truly "crystallizes," rejects those people who do not really harmonize with it, and attracts those people who truly complement each other. As with any art or sport, the first steps and experiences are the *least* rewarding and interesting, and the most difficult. The more one invests of oneself into this work, the more alive and rewarding it will become. Moreover, a certain period of time, commitment, and personal investment are necessary to have personally *lived results.*

The Second or Closing Phase of the operation of the

Generator does require a minimun amount of *practice* and *lived results* using the Opening Phase before one may proceed with the Closing Phase. This may generally take a year, or at least six months, except in particular cases where a person is already trained or has achieved a high level of consciousness and being. It also requires a minimum amount of intellectual, moral, and emotional stability and responsibility! Should these elementary rules be disregarded, one or two things will happen: either *nothing would happen* with the Generator, and the work would simply be done in a sterile, intellectual manner; or worse yet, many negative thoughts, feelings, drives, words, and deeds would become greatly amplified and intensified with the participant becoming much more powerful and effective for Evil and thus pave a direct road to "Hell" for himself/herself. For once the Generator is set up and does function in our Field of Consciousness, it will vivify, activate, and intensify *everything it comes in contact with, on any level, and without any regards for its "Good" or "Evil" consequences . . .*

This Second or Advanced operation of the Generator can go on *forever*, becoming *self-controlling* and *self-directing,* and can be used for countless *specific practical* purposes. This is because, at a certain point, the operator and the participants *open up their intuition* and become *guided from within* as to what to do and how to change or add new parts and aspects to its operation! This is where the *true, mature,* or *spiritual work* really begins: when a person, or group, is *guided from within* and has established its own *operational "contacts"* with the Other Side of Life, and is thus autonomous and independent of external authorities and guidance.

This Advanced Phase is made up of two basic aspects which could be viewed as a "Female" and a "Male" aspect. The Female aspect is called *Entering the Silence.* Its purpose is to gradually and systematically train and open up our *Sensitivity* and our *Receptivity,* first on the Physical/Etheric level, then on the Astral level and on the Mental level, and finally, for those who are ready and capable of functioning on this level, also on the Spiritual level. It involves "practicing Silence" on the four Planes of Being, each with a Male/Female polarity. Thus:

1. Beginning with the *Physical/Etheric* level, the participants should be silent (which is the Male aspect) and then they should *listen* to all the physical sounds that are present around and within them (the Female Aspect).

    Obviously this requires a lot of concentration, attention, thinking, and feeling. It tunes in the consciousness of the participant to his physical body and the physical plane, opening up his sensitivity and receptivity to that Plane of Being, as much as he is capable at that point.

2. The participants then move on to the *Astral/Emotional* level. Here they should seek to still their desires, yearnings, emotions, and feelings (the Male part of Emotional Silence) and then allow all their desires, yearnings, feelings, and emotions to flow freely through their Field of Consciousness, realizing that they have these desires and feelings, and many, many more . . . but that *they* are something much greater, much deeper, higher, and vaster than their feelings (this being the Female part of Emotional Silence).

    This also requires the use of the basic muscles of consciousness and tunes in the consciousness of the participants to his/her Astral Body and the Astral Plane, opening up his/her sensitivity and receptivity as much as he/she is capable of at that point.

3. Then we come to the *Mental* level where the procedure is, basically, the same as it was for the previous levels. Now the participants should strive to empty their minds of all thoughts and ideas (the Male part of Mental Silence) and then, realizing that they cannot do so effectively, they should allow all the thoughts and ideas that are present in and around them to flow freely through their Field of Consciousness, realizing that they have these thoughts and ideas, and many more, but that *they* are something much greater, deeper, higher, and vaster than their thoughts (the Female part of Mental Silence).

    This will train and develop other "muscles" and faculties of the Psyche and will tune in the consciousness of the participants to their Mental Body and the Mental Plane, opening up their sensitivity and receptivity as much as they are capable of at that point.

4. Finally, we have the *Spiritual level* where the polarities are now *inverted*, that is, where one begins with the Female aspect of Silence and concludes with the Male aspect of Silence. At this point, the participant should "listen to the Voice of Silence" which is the Voice of his Higher Self, pouring forth and manifesting through his Intuition!

    Should something happen or a message be received (and this could be in the form of an image, a symbol, a mental crystallization, words, feelings, or physical impulses), it should be properly assimilated and interpreted (the Female part of Silence).

    The Male part then consists of making a *firm commitment* to implement, in one's life and one's being, whatever has been received *no matter what the cost may be!* For, should the Intuition, or the Voice of Silence, speak to us, and we do not heed its message or guidance, it would simply remain silent for a while, no matter what attempts we make to reactivate it.

This process also requires the use of, and trains, different muscles and functions of our Psyche, and tunes our consciousness to our Spiritual Body and the Spiritual Plane, opening up our sensitivity and receptivity as much as possible to that Plane of Being.

At this point, the participants will have systematically tuned in their attention and activated their sensitivity and receptivity to the four Planes of Being. In the process, they will also have purified their Aura and activated their Psychospiritual Centers so that they will be in a state of maximum readiness, of maximum *Sensitivity* and *Receptivity*, for getting into the second major phase of the Advanced Operation of the Generator which is *Theurgy* or *Ritual* proper. Here, the central purpose will be simply to bring into the Field of Consciousness as much Light, Fire, and Life as possible through the use of Symbols, Images, and Rituals. For these will then act as Light and Consciousness "Transformers" and thereby bring through the spiritual energies of the Divine Spark.

Here, a proper understanding and practice of *The Nature and Use of Ritual for Spiritual Attainment* (Llewellyn Publications, 1985) is absolutely vital. For it is at this point that the seven fundamentals, discussed in the above-mentioned work, can be introduced as ritual into the Generator for Theurgic purposes.

First, a proper understanding and an "experiential acquaintance" with the nature and use of *Divine Names* is absolutely necessary to work with the *Sign of the Cross* which will be formulated three times and used in several formulae to activate core Psychospiritual Centers so as to raise their vibrations and energies, and *awaken the Great Cross of Light within one's Aura.*

Then the Trisagion*, the Lord's Prayer, and the Hail Mary can be used; and finally, the Nicene Creed, the Beatitudes, and the Ten Commandments can be introduced and "worked" systematically to decode their deeper meanings and implications, and to make them come alive in the consciousness, life, and being of the participants. Once Divine Names, the Sign of the Cross, and the Lord's Prayer have been *mastered* and *rendered alive* in one's consciousness and in the Circle, then many other interesting variations and developments can be introduced to amplify and direct the Light, the Energies, and the Materials so evoked.

To give one practical example: after the Opening Phase has been successfully concluded and that the participants have gone through "Entering the Silence" on the four Planes and are thus now at a point of maximum *Awareness, Sensitivity,* and *Receptivity,* the following Ritual can be used Theurgically:

> Vibrate the Divine Names of the Holy Trinity *three times* in your Aura by tracing three Signs of the Cross— the first time to bring Light and Power from the Spiritual Body to the Mental Body, suffusing it; the second time to bring Light and Power from the Mental Body to the Astral Body, suffusing it; and the third time to bring Light and Power from the Astral Body to the Etheric/Physical Body, suffusing it.

This procedure will awaken four key Psychospiritual Centers on the Tree of Life (Head, Heart, and Shoulders) and will do so in three basic Worlds or Dimensions:

---

*Not discussed in *The Nature and Use of Ritual for Spiritual Attainment* but which can be subjected to the same type of analysis and "work."

THE ASSIATIC (The Subconscious Mind)
THE YETZIRATIC (The Conscious Mind)
THE BRIATIC (The Superconscious Mind)

After the *Awakening Cross* is used to "switch on" the Light and Power in the Aura and Tree of Life of the Candidate, comes the *Cleansing Ritual* to purify his various bodies and their key Psychospiritual Centers with the following formula:

"O Lord, Cleanse Thou me a sinner, and have mercy
upon me"

Or something similar, which is said *three times* to bring Light and Power from the Spiritual to the Mental, Astral, and Etheric/Physical Bodies.

Then comes the *Consecrating Ritual* to raise and focus one's various energies, vibrations, and intentions which can be done through the formula:

"O Lord, open Thou my lips and my mouth shall show
forth Thy praise"

which is also said *three times* for the same reason.

At this point, the Generator Operator, or Group Leader, can ask the participants to project the Cross of Light from their own auras into the center of the circle of Light Generator and to expand the "arms" of this Cross, the vertical arms into the Heavens and into the center of the Earth, and the horizontal arms into the room (or even the community) by either visualizing a "horizontal shaft of Light" or by linking it with the Circle which is then expanded and enlarged.

Into the center of that Cross of Light, one or more of the Fundamentals can be vibrated Theurgically to awaken all of one's Psychospiritual Centers, to raise one's energy and vibration level to the highest possible point. These energies and materials can then be diffused and radiated into the psychic atmosphere of the community where the Generator is being operated and even into that of the whole world.

Into the center of that Cross of Light each of the participants can also project and visualize themselves, or a friend or relative in need of healing, guidance or inspiration, or yet a group of people, a particular city or place, or a nation. New Rituals, Meditations, or Psychospiritual Exercises can be devised and experimented with. Mental imagery, guided daydreams, and Inner Journeys, as well as "rising up the Planes" and Path Work can be done. The *Llewellyn Inner Guide Tapes* could also very profitably be integrated and used at this point as well as tapes that we will be producing for our readers. These tapes can be used again and again in the many ways described in Melita Denning and Osborne Phillips' *Magical States of Consciousness,* (Llewellyn Publications, 1985), so that the combination of Word, Sound, and Theurgy may evoke a rich tapestry of Images and Feelings culminating in a Soul-stirring Psychospiritual Drama. Specifically, they can be used for:

- Meditation and Inner experience of controlled changes in Consciousness.
- Soul Sculpture—the enhancement or overcoming of particular qualities in one's character.
- Initiation—a powerful program of psychospiritual transformation.
- Psychological Integration—establishing conscious relationships with the deeper levels of the Psyche and activating neural and etheric circuitry.
- Magical Procedures, as incorporated into Rites intended to bring about changes in the Outer, as well as the Inner Worlds.

The list is endless and depends essentially on the creative imagination and intuitive breakthroughs of the participants. Naturally, the faith of each one of the participants, their level of consciousness and being, the amount of time and dedication that is given to activating and making the

Generator "come alive" and "speak" will determine the results that will be obtained. These results and the Generator's efficiency should grow and amplify to unsuspected heights and depths with the passage of time and with repeated practice which will demonstrate *experientially* to the participants that the Spiritual Adventure is, indeed, the Ultimate and Greatest Adventure . . . because it leads one to the very center and core of one's being, of Reality, and to the very *Source of Life!*

3
GROUP WORK

*The Nature and Use of the Group Mind
and Energies for Spiritual Attainment*

The central and original contribution of this work, in addition
to practically expanding and developing the perspective
and exercises suggested in *The Nature and Use of Ritual for
Spiritual Attainment* for the psychospiritual growth of the
Candidate, is the introduction of Group Work, or the Operation of an Energy, Consciousness, and Light Generator.
This Generator, as we have seen in the previous chapter,
consists essentially of forming and working in a *Circle of
Light*. The addition of this most important tool goes to the
very heart of the Sacred Traditions which have always
claimed that authentic psychospiritual work is based on
two central axes: the vertical one or *Love of God* through
Worship, and the horizontal one or *Love of Man* through *Service;* the Quest for *Yod He Vau He* and the Building of the
Temple of Solomon; the Search for Christ and the Building
of His Church; *Upaya* and *Satsang,* the practice of spiritual
exercises and the establishment of a community . . . and
many other such names which all point to the same
Reality.

It is not by accident that the greatest spiritual thinkers
of our times, together with leading social scientists, have
seen Group Work as what "history now demands of us" and

as constituting the next basic step, or quantum leap in human and spiritual evolution. Thus, Sri Aurobindo and Theilard de Chardin, Pitirim Sorokin and Arnold Toynbee, Dion Fortune and William Gray, Roberto Assagioli and Alice Bailey and the Tibetan, to mention just a few prominent writers, have all called for a realization of what Group Work could do for humankind and its implementation in our daily lives. It is, likewise, not by accident if all kinds of intentional groups, spiritual associations, and esoteric organizations have sprung up like mushrooms all over the world and particularly in the USA! Political Science, Social Psychology, and Sociology are the modern academic disciplines that have focused their attention upon the study of Group Behavior—its causes, dynamics, and consequences. All three take it for granted today that Man is a Social Being and that human interaction is absolutely vital for the survival, well-being, and continued growth of a human being as have the religious and spiritual Traditions of the past!

This is what two of the best known writers have to say about the nature, dynamics, and functions of Group Work for the modern Candidate to spiritual awakening. Thus writes Roberto Assagioli:

> This law (that of Group Endeavor or Group Work) can be considered as the *outstanding law of the New Age.* But the first thing to be realized is that the New Age groups will be quite different in character from those which have existed until now. The authoritarian attitude of the leader at the center belongs to the past, and the groups of the New Age will be *free association of individuals* held together by a *common idea,* a *common purpose,* and *common service.* The pattern of such groups will no longer be that of a solar system with a great center of light and lesser units revolving around it; it will be much more like *a constellation of stars* or suns proceeding unitedly toward a *common goal.*
>
> This calls for a high standard of integration and

mutual dedication to the objective of the group by its members, which is something that can only be arrived at through *inner,* unanimous orientation. This is a very different thing from outer imposed discipline, and to understand how it may be arrived at a brief survey of how a group is constituted may be helpful.

First it should be realized that a group—a coalescence of individuals—forms in itself a *living entity.* This is a difficult concept for our objective minds which are accustomed to associate each living being with a corresponding separate and visible body. But if we examine the analogy of a nation or of a human being, it becomes clear that the interplay and blending of the units constitutes a *whole,* which, in turn, becomes a living qualitative, purposeful entity, composed of the sum total of its parts and existing through them as a manifesting force.

In this way nations, tribes, families, and all kinds of collectivities of people constitute *group entities,* as also do the more temporary groupings like assemblies, audiences, and teams. It is an acknowledged fact that when two or more people come together, their mutual interplay starts a process of coalescence which results in a *new combination,* as in the process of chemistry. In other words, group life of some kind begins to take form. This is easily seen when a crowd gathers for some specific purpose; it often integrates rapidly and its "mood" develops and changes. Sometimes powerful and dramatic happenings result. A group entity is composed of all the constituent parts of which we, as human beings with all our different aspects, are composed. It has a *spirit,* which is its integrating purpose; a *soul* or qualitative aspect; a *mental* aspect and an emotional aspect, which are made up of the blended mental and emotional aspects of its members; and a *physical* manifestation through its outer organization and its activities All these form in time a "group personality," and to really know and understand a group we should attempt to recognize each of these parts of its make-up, just as we need to in ourselves.

The inner, spontaneous integration of the New Age groups grows primarily out of their *united purpose.* These groups are not formed for the betterment of the individual members, but have a greater purpose than themselves, an objective which the individuals could not reach alone and which shines out before them as a magnetic and compelling goal. That objective or purpose may be to meet the need of some section of humanity, to establish some idea or ideal, or to lift some of the burden that oppresses men, but no matter what its nature it will be for the good of a greater number.

This is the basic purpose of the Law of Group Endeavor—the elevation of the whole—which in the past has been attempted individually, but now can be brought about more *rapidly* by our combining together in group work. The power of united effort upon the physical plane is being recognized today on a large scale. The power of united emotion is also being recognized and is often exploited—as well as feared. But the power of *united thought* has been little grasped as yet. This, however, must and will be the great New Age mode of *creative action.*

Group work of this type necessitates considerable *self-discipline.* The individuality, while its qualities are needed when blended in the whole, must be so merged in the united purpose that it is not individualistic in expression, or attached to its own freedom, as even freedom may become a glamour. Personality differences should not be allowed to cut across or outweigh the group purpose or dominate the group life. Such qualities as love, tolerance, understanding and service need cultivation and deliberate use, while criticism, self-assertion, indifference, and other separative tendencies call for a constant vigilance so that they may be offset.

Group relationship calls for skill and sacrifice, but its techniques are rapidly being assimilated and worked with by many who are coming under the impulse of Group Endeavor. These men and women are establishing the growing science of human relations, and there is continual indication in every field of the usefulness, the power for good, and the increasing growth of these group forms of activity and endeavor. (*Meditation for the New Age,* First Year, Set III, pp. 14-16).

And he concludes:

The development of self-awareness can rightfully be called a scientific process, because it can be based on observation, experience, and experimentation, without any preconceived ideas or beliefs. It starts with a direct and primary experience, namely *awareness* of the conscious existence of oneself as a human being. From this fundamental fact of experience one is naturally urged to investigate the nature and the constitution of the human being, the psychological anatomy and physiology, so to speak. Then one proceeds to man's vital connections with other human beings and with supra-personal Reality, because self-awareness constitutes only the *first* stage. It is not sufficient to realize our personal separate self-identity; it does not satisfy, and may even arouse a sense of anguish. The steps of the ladder, or stages through which one can reach up, recognize, and experience spiritual realities can be indicated in the following way:

1. Finding oneself
2. Finding the Self
3. Finding other Selves
4. Finding the One Self—The Universal Being, the Supreme Reality. (*Meditation for the New Age*, Second Year, Set III, pp. 4-5).

Alice Bailey and the Tibetan tell us:

A disciple is one who is beginning to comprehend group work, and to change his center of activity from himself (as the pivot around which everything revolves) to the group center. (*Initiation, Human and Solar*, Lucis Trust, pp. 4-5).

And:

Let the disciple merge himself within the circle of his other selves. Let but one colour blend them and their unity appear. Only when the group is known and sensed can *energy be wisely emanated.*

One thing all disciples and applicants for initiation have to do is to *find that particular group of servers to which they belong on the inner plane,* to recognise them upon the physical plane, and to unite with them in service for the race. This recognition will be based upon:

   a.   Unity of aim.
   b.   Oneness in vibration.
   c.   Identity in group affiliation.
   d.   Karmic links of long standing.
   e.   Ability to work in harmonious relation.

Superficially, this may appear one of the easiest of the rules, but in practice it is not so. Mistakes are easily made, and the problem of working harmoniously in group alignment is not so simple as it may appear. Egoic vibration and relationship may exist, yet the outer personalities may not harmonise. It is the work, then, of the applicant to strengthen the grip of his Ego upon his personality, so that the esoteric group relation may become possible upon the physical plane. He will do so by the disciplining of his own personality, and not by the correction of his brothers. (Ibid, pp. 202-03).

Finally, they conclude:

Regard, therefore, *all your work as group work*, causing effects which are inevitable and contributing to the potency of the group thought form ... Every group in the world is a nucleus for the focusing and interplay of the *seven types of force*, just as every human being is also a meeting place for *the seven types of energy*—two in the ascendant and five less potent. Every group can consequently be a creative center and produce that which is an expression of the controlling energies and of the directed thought of the thinkers of the group. From the standpoint of Those Who see and guide, therefore, *every group is constructing something* that is relatively tangible and governed by certain building laws. The great work of the Builders proceeds steadily. Often that which is built is inchoate, futile and without form or purpose, and of no use to either gods or men.

But the race as a whole is now coming into an era wherein the mind is becoming a potent factor; many are learning to hold the mind steady in the light, and consequently are receptive to ideas hitherto unrecognised. If a group of minds can be so drawn together and fused into an adequate synthesis, and if they (in their individual and daily meditation) keep focused or oriented towards that which can be apprehended, great concepts can be grasped and great ideas intuited. Men can train themselves—as a group—to think these intuited ideas of the true and the beautiful and of the Plan into manifested existence, and thus a *creation of beauty, embodying a divine principle, can be built.* Ponder on this, seek to fit yourself for the registering of these ideas, and train yourselves to formulate them into thoughts and to transmit them so that others can apprehend them also. This is the nature of the real work to be done by the new groups, and students today who can grasp this idea have the opportunity to do some of this pioneering work. (*Esoteric Psychology*, Lucis Trust, pp. 10-12).

Several other such passages could be cited, from these or other authors, all pointing to the same reality. What I shall now attempt to do is to summarize these principles and to deduce their practical applications for you, the reader and possible Candidate.

For the Buddhist, representing one of the great Eastern Spiritual Traditions, personal transformation and the spiritual life rest on two fundamental activities: *Upaya* and *Satsang*. *Upaya* is the carrying out of various psychospiritual exercises: Meditation, Chanting, Contemplation, and the like, which could be performed *alone*, in *a group*, or *both*. *Satsang* is the formation of an intentional community, of a group dedicated to spiritual work. Hence, in the East, the nature and importance of Group Work was well recognized and given traditional sanction.

In the Western Spiritual Tradition we find the same basic truth but couched in different words. Here, the essence of the spiritual life rests upon the *Worship of God* and *the Building of His Church*. The Worship of God entails becoming aware of, making contact with, and drawing down into one's consciousness and being the Divine Light, Fire, and

Life. Whereas the Building of His Church consists both of perfecting one's personality, so as to offer it as "His Temple of manifestation in the material world," and of establishing an intentional community or a "Spiritual family" with whom to share part of one's life and to worship. Again, we find the same pattern of doing *personal work* and *group work* in a cyclical fashion to complement and complete each other.

In the religious and monastic traditions and communities, this double thrust and recognition of personal and group work is manifested even more clearly: all of them have their prescribed personal devotions and group worship with the community as the main support and receptacle for the work that is being done.

If we look at the various Psychic, Pagan, and Witchcraft Tradition, this principle becomes even more obvious: they all have their particular teachings, personal work, and group work with the Coven or Grove as the "operational channel" for their psychic transformations, the raising of power, and the carrying out of their selected work. The Coven, or the Group, is absolutely vital to achieve the chosen results.

The same may be said of the various Occult, Mystical, and Magical Orders, the Rosicrucian, Hermetic, or Alchemical Traditions: they also have work that must be done regularly by the Candidate alone and work that can only be done in the Temple or Lodge as group work.

Thus, we find the same principle in operation, but with different explanations and justifications being given by each Tradition and Group. While the individual can and must do much work by himself, some work can only be done and must be done within the context of a group, whether this group is called a Church, a Temple, an Intentional Community, a Coven, a Grove, or a Lodge matters little.

To gain deeper knowledge and understanding of the inner dynamics of this principle, let us for a moment turn to modern Sociology. Sociology teaches quite clearly as two of its most fundamental premises that "Man is a social being" and that "Human Interaction brings about a creative psychic synthesis." To say that "Man is a social being" is to say that: in order to be born, in order to survive, and in order to further develop and actualize himself, a human being needs interaction on the three great levels of being: the physical, the human, and the spiritual. The main assumption of modern Sociology is thus that Man is not a solitary being, that the Psyche is an "organ of interaction," and that Man must live, work and have his being with other human beings. I have summarized this basic sociological teaching by simply saying to my sociology students that:

What food is to the body, human interaction is to the psyche, and prayer is to the soul.

If we do not eat physical food, we will starve physically; if we do not interact with others, we will starve our consciousness developing a whole panoply of symptoms such as fatigue, depression, boredom, a high level of irritability and frustration, a sense of self-loss, and a loss of our meaning and purpose in life (this question is fully developed in my "Love-Vitamin theory")' and if we do not pray (or consciously draw into our consciousness and being the Divine Light, Fire, and Life), once we have awakened our spiritual consciousness, it will "fall asleep" again and our Soul will starve!

To say that "Human Interaction brings about a creative psychic synthesis" means essentially this:

When two or more human beings interact with each other, it is not their *bodies* that interact but their *consciousness, and specifically, we have an exchange here between mind and mind, heart and heart,* and *will and will.* This triple interaction or exchange is *creative* in that it generates new ideas, gives birth to new feelings, and releases new energies. Hence, human interaction can, sociologically, be seen as the very fountainhead of our *human* life, as the crucible whence new intellectual, emotional, and vital energies and forces are activated.

Finally, modern Sociology tells us clearly that:

Human Interaction is a far more complex process than is generally assumed because we interact or exchange energies and materials on three basic levels:

a. At the *conscious level,* we exchange and transact images, words, and deeds.
b. At the *subconscious level,* we exchange and transact subliminally energies and biopsychic materials.
c. At the *superconscious* level, we exchange and transact superliminally energies and psychospiritual materials.

If we now move on to the perspective of Psychosynthesis for further insights into the nature and dynamics of Group Work we find the following:

The entire process of Psychosynthesis as a method of psychotherapy moves through three distinct phases which are: *Personal* Psychosynthesis, *Interpersonal* Psychosynthesis, and *Transpersonal* Psychosynthesis, clearly pointing to the importance and role of group work and human relations in the entire process.

Personal Psychosynthesis basically involves acquiring systematic self-knowledge, self-mastery, and self-integration. One begins with an exploration of the Field of Consciousness and its 7 functions, then one moves to an exploration of the Preconscious, Subconscious, Unconscious and finally, the Superconscious. One continues by learning how to harness, direct, coordinate and express all the energies, faculties, and resources of one's being. Finally, one completes this process by integrating one's entire being—physical, psychological, and spiritual—which is the "intraspsychic marriage" of the personality with the Soul. Interpersonal

Psychosynthesis involves knowing other types of human beings, after having known one's self, and learning how to establish *right relationships* with them, how to be able to meet common needs and to work together to realize common ideals.

Transpersonal Psychosynthesis involves knowing the Self, the Divine Spark in oneself and in others, and how to establish right relationships with that Self.

With the foregoing as a preliminary foundation, we are now ready to approach Group Work as suggested by the creation and operation of our Energy, Consciousness, and Light Generator which, by its very title, describes its essential function. As I have mentioned before, the reader/Candidate does not *immediately* need an "operational Group" to carry out the work outlined in this book. There is much intellectual and practical work that he can do *before* he joins or forms such a group and that he can do *after* he has joined such a group, but in its absence. There is, however, a right time and set of conditions for *joining* or *forming* such a group with much important and productive work that can only be done within the context that the group provides. For the group does, indeed, add something invaluable and offer its unique elements! Finally, there is also a time when the reader/Candidate can again work alone, after he has participated in the Circle of Light Generator, which may or may not still exist. Here, the Candidate can go through the motions, circulate the Light, and go through the Rituals within his own Inner Temple (that of his Aura and Tree of Life), in his *imagination*, and telepathically contact and invoke the others . . . or in the Greater Inner Plane Temple when he is capable of ascending there or is given entry therein.

Briefly put, what are the psychospiritual advantages and dynamics of having a Circle of Light Generator? These are many; some are quite obvious and others more subtle. These are:

1. Each person has a multiple-layer Energy Field and a Tree of Life, which are pulsating and radiating various energies and bio-psycho-spiritual materials that *can enter into relationship with each other, bringing about a variety of exchanges that are very important for one's state of consciousness and growth.* Thus there is an Etheric, Astral, Mental, and perhaps, an emerging Spiritual Aura. Within this Aura, or Energy Field, is located the Tree of Life with its 10 Spheres, 7 of which are truly functional and can be fully activated while a human being is on Earth, namely: Chesed, Geburah, Tiphareth, Netzach, Hod, Yesod, and Malkuth.

    If a minimum of 7 persons is required to have an "operational Group," it is precisely because each person, at a certain point, *becomes a Channel and a Focal Point for the energies and materials of one of these 7 Spheres.* Hence, were there but 6 persons in the Generator, one essential type of Light and Energy would be missing! To have more than 13 or 14 persons in the Generator would also *diffuse* and *dissipate* some of the Energies and Materials that are being brought through. Ideally, when the Generator has grown up to 14 persons, it can now be split up into two separate Generators of 7 persons each. Please bear in mind, dear reader/Candidate, that these are not hard rules "bound in cement" but general guidelines. The final decision must always be *yours* and that of the persons you might be working with!

2. Most of us, most of the time, are not vitally emotionally, or mentally balanced and we feel tired and uncreative. When we operate our Circle of

Light Generator, we have an excellent *natural* and *integral* way of bringing *Peace* and *Life* to ourselves which, otherwise, we would find very hard to achieve. The Opening Phase of the operation of the Generator allows each participant to draw on the *collective energies* which are thus generated, in their Female expression as *relaxation* (Peace) and in their Male expression as *Simulation* (Life), to systematically relax their bodies, emotions, and minds, and then to stimulate their imagination, feelings, thoughts, and intuitions. In this fashion, participants are able to *balance* and *recharge* themselves in the three worlds and to exchange what I call "Love-Vitamins"; all of which are most important in setting up the ideal conditions for doing the true psychospiritual work that will follow. It is, of course, possible to balance, recharge, relax and stimulate oneself in other ways to achieve that proper alignment and openness to the Inner Bodies, Centers, and Energies, but this is a simple, natural, and time-proven way of doing that.

3. It is a fundamental postulate of the modern sciences that "the whole is greater than the sum of its parts" and that "bringing different elements together in a *synthesis* is always a creative process." Thus, when we have several human beings bringing their own particular vibrations, energies, and psychospiritual materials—their distinctive *"Lights"*— the blending and interaction between them brings about new quantitative and qualitative elements that are more than the sum of their individual parts. A new *reality* is literally generated and brought about—the *Egregor*, the "Psychic Atmosphere," or the "Group Soul." The physical manifestation of this entity is, naturally, the persons composing the

Circle of Light and the Circle itself. On the Etheric, Astral, Mental, and Spiritual levels a new *being* is engendered for which the physical persons are the cells and the Circle the organism. Such a Being is given birth to, fed, and further developed by the collective energies and vibrations of the Circle— by its composite "Lights." But, in turn, it can also feed it, stimulate it, and elevate it to new heights. At a further point in the psychospiritual development of its members, it can become the "transducer" or "transformer" between the physical and the human worlds and the psychic and spiritual worlds, allowing mutual and very enriching exchanges to take place—Light, Fire, and Life to flow downwards, and Consciousness and Experience to flow upwards. Thus what the Symbol and the Telesmatic Image is to the individual, the Circle and its Egregor is to the Group!

4. In forming and operating a growth, or spiritual-work Group, most people think that they are dealing only with the physical location and the persons, the psychological and psychic energies, and the spiritual Light that are involved. This, actually, is only half the story! For every "Operational Group" on the *physical Plane* there also forms a corresponding Group in the *Inner Planes*, made up of psychic and spiritual entities which are "on the same wave-length" and drawn to the same ideal. It is here that Angels, Masters, and more evolved Beings, "our Brothers and Sisters from the Stars" can come and visit us in a very real and tangible though non-physical way! St. Paul correctly stated that, at all times, we are all surrounded by a "Cloud of Invisible Witnesses," beings on the Inner Planes who are drawn to us by the Light, Energies, and Vibrations

we radiate. The same, of course, is also true and even *more* true for intentional groups focusing their thoughts, feelings, and vitality on some common Ritual or Purpose. Here, it is the Egregor, or "Psychic Atmosphere" of the Group, the new Evolutionary Being we have collectively given birth to in the Inner Worlds, that becomes the "interface" or "Door" through which the human can communicate with the spiritual and vice versa. It is also the "'channel" through which we can enter the "Communication of Saints" where the duality of "This Side of Life and the Other Side" disappear to give place to *life eternal* with no Death and no Separation . . . Herein also lies the true and healthy "communication with the Dead" and the "Passport to the Inner Worlds—the Spiritport"!

5. Thus the New Age Group, in our case the Circle of Light Generator, also becomes the "Temple of God," the "Church of Christ," the personal interpersonal, and transpersonal structure or organism which links God and Nature, Spirit and Matter, Man and God. It is the New Being to which we all have to give personal and collective birth and which constitutes the next "quantum leap" in our human and spiritual evolution. It is this "Temple of the Living God" that will truly connect "Heaven and Earth," the physical and the spiritual side, and the outer Sanctuary with the Inner Sanctuary wherein Angels, the Master, and the Divine Light dwell. More cannot be said in words and must be *personally experienced* to be truly fathomed and understood.

6. The basic function of the Generator or Group Work is to *intensify, amplify,* and *enrich*, both quantitatively and qualitatively, *whatever* is being

done, thought, felt, imagined, intuited, or exprienced by the individual and by the Group. Thus the Generator functions not only as a *Transformer* but also as an *Amplifier* of Consciousness and Life for the individual. And it allows a most important process to occur: by being intensified, amplified, and enriched, materials which would normally lie either in the Subconscious/Unconscious or in the Superconscious are now *able to penetrate into the field of consciousness* ... and the Unconscious is thus *made conscious* (which, by the way, is one of the main functions of group therapy but on a lower level!).

7. Jesus said: "Whenever two or three of you shall be assembled in my name, there I shall be amongst them" thereby pointing to a profound spiritual *reality* and *mystery* to which we can only point in intellectual words and which must be *experienced and lived* to be understood. By forming a Circle of Light Generator and using the Mass, or its functional equivalent, in its Advanced Phase, we are setting up *in ourselves* and *in our midst*, in the Circle of Light.and its Egregor, the *Outer and Inner Temple* whereby to *consciously commune with the Living Christ*, to absorb and assimilate His *Light, Fire, and Life* to raise our consciousness and "redeem ourselves and the world" (this point will be elaborated and analyzed in much greater details in a later book describing the spiritual aspects of the Church and the Mass). We are also creating a "funnel" or a "channel of Manifestation" for His Spirit to enter into and act in the world. For it is here that the outer and the Inner Temple come together, that Heaven is linked with the Earth, that Man and God are reconciled, and that "the ends, spiritual and

physical, finally meet" . . . as a New Creature is
born *in, around,* and *above us,* interpenetrating us
and manifesting through us on *all Planes of Being.*
But I speak of an *experience* and a *mystery* which
you, the reader and Candidate, must discover for
yourself!

To conclude this section, let me briefly share with you
what such a Circle of Light Generator has done for me and
what vital functions it has performed for me at one very
critical point in my life. For several years, I had been
organizing and leading Generators in the city where I lived
and in other cities in the U.S. and Canada. Thus I had
several "operational" Circle of Light Generators functioning
on different levels with different types of people, some at
the elementary and a few at the intermediary levels. Then,
the "hour of destiny" struck for me; I had an appointment
with fate, as it were, and the biggest crisis (and spiritual
test!) of my life hit me. Physically, emotionally, and
mentally, I was utterly devastated, lingering for a long time
between life and death, sanity and insanity, coping with
everyday life or letting go . . . It is then that I discovered
many aspects and functions of the Generator that I would
never have suspected before, and that new layers and pos-
sibilites were *experientially* revealed to me.

Whenever I would lead or participate in the activities
of a Circle (I had several of them functioning and I kept
going to them out of a sheer sense of "duty"), after the
Opening Phase, I would suddenly find myself again—find
the Self I had lost! There, for a few moments, my *mind,* my
heart, and my *will* could function again and I would emerge
from the Astral Sea of Emotions that, most of the time,
enveloped me and engulfed me, tossing me hither and
thither in an ocean of pain and confusion. It is during those
short but most precious moments that I acquired the *higher
perspective,* the *proper measure,* to understand what was

happening to me and what was *required of me,* as well as the strength to *do it* and the *love* to *motivate me to go on living.* It is also at that point that I realized that one special Circle of Light had become my *living Noah's Ark,* to see me through the "Deluge" of the greatest crisis of my life . . . and that it could do the same for others, for *you,* the reader and the Candidate!

From this experience, I now perceived new functions, usages, and possibilities for the Generator which had been "revealed" to me and which I had put together . . . many years earlier! . . . never guessing in my wildest imagination that it would, some day, save my life and my sanity, and give me the Light and Strength to go on Living! Indeed, such Group Work and the operation of a "live Generator" can function as the *Noah's Ark,* into the New Age and through the Great Tribulation of the end of this Century.

When the Candidate has reached the point where he/she feels that the time has come for having such an operational Generator but that he/she is not yet part of one, how can he/she proceed? The first step is, of course, *knowing oneself* and knowing what one truly wants for oneself at that point in time. The second step is *to know* and to *have practiced alone* most of the materials and techniques suggested in this book. Connected with this is setting up one's own personal *library* and *Sanctuary,* keeping a *diary* and a *workbook,* and *doing the daily work.*

The third and fundamental step is to grow, humanly and spiritually, to raise one's level of consciousness and vibrations, and to change one's level of being. It is here that the theoretical perspective and the practical exercises presented in *The Nature and Use of Ritual for Spiritual Attainment,* and their further developments and "operationalization" in the present book, or in similar books of the Llewellyn Spiritual Sciences Series, or even in other works of the same type, can be *invaluable.*

Today, one of the great "novelties" and opportunities of our times is precisely that such "Arcane Knowlege" with detailed psychospiritual exercises is available to the public as never before and can be found without too much effort or expense. There are also a variety of valid groups and organizations which, with a little "common sense" and "spiritual discernment," can provide the *elementary training* for such personal work and growth. What is still needed, however, and what can ultimately come only from the *depths of the heart* of the Candidate and from the *heights of his own consciousness and being* are:

The motivation or love for the work and the actual work, efforts, and sacrifices which are required!

The fourth step is to become a "living magnet" for drawing the right conditions and *persons* to oneself; something which occurs naturally and automatically once a person has activated, purified, and consecrated his Aura and Psychospiritual Centers to a certain degree. And this can be done *alone*, under the guidance of one or more teachers, and with or without a group or an organization.

The fifth step is to provide objective and effective *Service* to others to complement on the horizontal level, the work of *Worship* on the vertical. This so as to make the Light, Fire, and Life, the insights and the energies, received through *Worship* to flow through one's being and to manifest themselves in the world. It is to show a kind heart, a good will, and a genuine interest in the growth and welfare of those one is connected to or has a relationship with.

The sixth step is to then visualize an "operational" Circle of Light Generator and to regularly and diligently *do the work* suggested by this book in one's *imagination.* The seventh and final step is to actually *join* an already existing and functioning Generator or to slowly *create* one. If one were to decide to create such a Generator, the basic steps are, again, quite simple:

a. One could propose this project to a few interested friends or persons one already knows; to discuss with them the theoretical perspective involved and to make sure that they understand the practical nature and dynamics of the work proposed.

b. Then one can form a little group, meet at regular times, and *experiment* with the Opening Phase of the operation of the Generator. At first, one could use it as a Love-Vitamin Generator to bring systematic Peace and Life to oneself and to the other members and let all the persons involved *discover the results and benefits accruing from such work.* Then this could be expanded for healing, inspirational, or other practical purposes, both for the group members and for others in the community, and *see what happens.*

c. Finally, one can then move towards the actual formation of an "operational" Generator with specific intermediate and long-range objectives such as the activation of one's intuition, the discovery of one's purpose and work in life, and the decoding and rendering "alive" certain Symbols, Images, and Rituals of one's religious or spiritual Tradition (of which the ones suggested in this work are mere basic examples). From here, the Path is open, many great practical possibilities will present themselves, and the Candidate can then engage in serious and sequential work producing tangible and verifiable transformations and results. Most important, at this point the Candidate *will know what he/she must do and do it!*

A little practical experimentation and actual work with the Generator will soon reveal and show the Candidate some of the basic features, dynamics and consequences of doing Group Work, what can and must be done *alone* and what can and must be done with a Group.

4
THE INNER SANCTUARY

*Founding and Constructing Your
Own Inner and Outer Sanctuary and Temple*

When approaching serious and mature psychospiritual training, personal transformation, and spiritual awakening, these questions are generally asked by Candidates (and rightly so!):

Should I build a "personal" Temple and Sanctuary?

Should the group I am working with, the Circle-Generator, construct a Temple and a Sanctuary in a specially set-aside and consecrated room?

Should I attend Church Services or the Ritualistic Convocations of an esoteric group or Spiritual Brotherhood?

What really constitutes the essential aspects of a true and living Temple and Sanctuary?

This chapter has been developed to answer legitimate questions such as these from the perspective of the

Spiritual Tradition and of my own personal experience. Herein, we shall set forth the fundamental insights and teachings that pertain to the proper understanding, construction, and utilization of an "operational" Temple and Sanctuary, specifically:

A. The building and unfoldment of the *inner, living* Human Temple and Sanctuary,

B. The construction and use of one's own personal, "home" Temple and Sanctuary,

C. The proper understanding and use of an established Temple or Church of one's religion,

D. The proper understanding and use of a Temple belonging to an esoteric group or Spiritual Brotherhood.

Let it be clearly and emphatically stated at the very onset of this chapter that all external, physical, collective temples and churches with their sanctuaries are in fact, nothing but external, physical projections, crystallizations, and symbolic representations of the One, Inner, Living Human Temple and Sanctuary of which the latter are, at best, partial, imperfect homologues.

From time immemorial and in *all* Sacred Traditions worthy of this name, the external, physical Temple and Sanctuary have always been constructed and used as a homologue and reminder of the inner living Human Temple and Sanctuay, so that by degrees, and according to one's level of consciousness and being, one could set forth upon the Great Work of Purifying, Consecrating, and preparing the Inner Temple and Sanctuary for the Coming and Manifestation of the Divine Spark.

In simple practical terms, this means that when one constructs an outer physical Temple and Sanctuary, and enters one to worship therein, and when one organizes and perceives one's life *as a living ritual,* only then is one really unfolding, nourishing, and worshipping in the Inner Temple and Sanctuary for then the ancient proverb comes true:

"As Above so Below, and as Below so Above."

These two processes, while seemingly quite different and using very different Principles and Materials (the first being *material* and in the world, while the second being *psychospiritual* and in one's consciousness) are exact *analogues* of each other, the first being the *symbol* and the means to the second which is the *living reality* and the end.

What is a *Temple,* whether it be an inner or outer one, and what role does a *Sanctuary* play in a *Temple* ?

A Temple is simply an organized structure of Matter and Energy (or Form and Force) designed to enable the *Spirit,* that which is Infinite, Timeless, and Formless, to manifest Itself and express Its Attributes in the Worlds of Creation that are finite and bound by time and form; it is a "creation" which enables the Creator to manifest as Consciousness, Love, and Life in the larger Creation which He has emanated; thus it is in essence, a complex, powerful and living *transformer* and *transducer* of Light, Fire, and Life unfolding and producing Consciousness.

A *Sanctuary* is simply the heart or core of the Temple, a small Temple within the Larger Temple, or a Prism for the Light, Fire and Life of the Spirit which acts as the "main switch" of the whole system, "stepping down" the psycho-spiritual Energies and "stepping up" the biospsychic energies so that *love* may emerge out of the unfolding consciousness. *It is the heart of the structure which enables a soul to be born and to manifest.*

As such, a Temple, both the Living Human Temple and its many representations, projections, and objectifications, is composed of certain essential component parts, which are:

a.   Various Fields of Energy and Matter ("Force" and

"Form") which compose what is generally called the *Aura*.

There are seven fields of Energy and Matter, according to the great Spiritual Traditions:

1. Physical and Etheric
2. Lower Astral
3. Higher Astral
4. Lower Mental
5. Higher Mental
6. Lower Spiritual
7. Higher Spiritual

which correspond to the Seven Planes of Creation. These are also known as the "Seven Bodies" of Man.

b. Then comes the Tree of Life and the Psychospiritual Centers (which act as "prisms" or "transformers" of the Divine Light, Fire and Life) which are Ten in number, but only Seven can be activated and attained while incarnate on this Earth, with an Eleventh Center that is in the process of formation. These are also known as the Seven Chakras of the Etheric Body of the Eastern Tradition, and the lower Seven Sephiroth of the Western Traditions, all of which have their roots in the Four Worlds of Creation: Physical, Astral, Mental, and Spiritual.*

c. Next we have the Seven Colors of the Spectrum of physical Light, that are associated with the Seven Psychospiritual Centers, and which are emanations and vibrations of Energy and Consciousness. These colors are

---

*For those who are concerned with understanding the distinctions and relationships between the Eastern Chakras and the Western Sephiroth, it can be pointed out that the 7 Eastern Chakras refer to the etheric body, whereas the 10 Western Sephiroth refer to the astral, mental and spiritual body.

A correlation can be made (and has been made by several authors) between the Eastern chakras and the Western Sephiroth so that the chakras can be polarized on the right and left pillars with the corresponding Sephiroth. Let it also be remembered that in the Eastern tradition there are more than the 7 Chakras. The Eastern Chakras really refer to the psychospiritual centers or the Sephiroth on the Middle Pillars which are then balanced by the Sephiroth on the right-hand pillar and the left-hand pillar.

Red, Orange, Yellow, Green , Blue, Indigo, Violet.

    d.   Then comes the Four Cardinal Points associated with the Four Elements and the Four Archangels. These are:

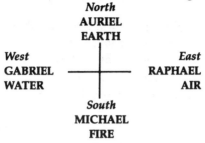

North
AURIEL
EARTH

West   *East*
GABRIEL   **RAPHAEL**
WATER   **AIR**

South
MICHAEL
FIRE

    e.   Finally, come the Seven Functions of the Psyche, with their associated psychological processes or what we have termed the "muscles of human consciousness":

Willing	**Concentration**
Thinking	**Meditation**
Feeling	**Devotion**
Intuition	**Invocation/Evocation**
Imagination	**Visualization**
Biopsychic Drives	**Energy Transformation and Direction**
Sensations	**Inner Observation**

Each of these can be represented by certain symbols, objects and colors.

    The particular organization of the Temple and Its Sanctuary with their related symbols, objects, and colors represents the specific intention or work for which it is dedicated and which is carried out through the various Rituals that are to be performed therein.

    Keep in mind that in all cases the Temple and its Sanctuary represent the *psychospiritual anatomy and physiology* of *human nature* so that whenever the Candidate enters his Temple or Sanctuary, he must *experientially enter into his own* psyche and consciousness, and that whatever is done in the Temple or Sanctuary must be deciphered in terms of its symbolism and then *done within himself or herself.*

A. The building and unfoldment of the inner living Human Temple and Sanctuary.

This is the true, essential, and living Temple of which all other Temples are but symbols, or an externalized projection, and for which they act as a "training gymnasium or laboratory."

The legendary Temple of Solomon, the true Church of Christ, and the Temple of the Mysteries were all archetypes and prototypes of that "Temple in Heaven not made with human hands" of which Jesus spoke when He said that He would rebuild it in three days . . .

The building and unfoldment of this Living Temple is accomplished through *living everyday life,* while realizing that all its experiences and tests are for our unfoldment, and through the love of God, Who is the ultimate Reality and highest Good, and finally, through the love of one's fellow Pilgrims, the human beings who cross our path.

The growth and completion of this living Temple can be consciously directed and accelerated by doing the Great Work and thereby undergoing a psychospiritual transformation.

Our *objective* actions, words, desires, feelings and thoughts in the outer world all have their immediate subjective repercussions in our Psyche, either by expanding or contracting our consciousness, for ascending into the Superconscious or descending into the Unconscious, and for regeneration or degeneration. This is why our daily attitudes and the cultivation of peace of mind, *serenity,* and the enfleshment of the basic virtues are more important than the psycho-spiritual exercises we perform occasionally!

The Foundation of our Temple and Sanctuary is a *wholesome, balanced, moral* and *productive life.*

The "Stones" are the virtues we practice daily and thus incarnate by incorporating them into our character.

The basic "Materials" and "Fuel" are unconditional love and good will manifested in our daily relationships.

The "Entrance" is the *ascending* Path of the Tree of Life leading to heightened states of consciousness and the ever-growing realization of our essential oneness.

The overall structure of this Temple and Sanctuary is grounded in the *Love of God*, or Worship, and in the *Love of Man*, or Service.

The *body* of the Human Temple is our biological organism or physical body which we feed through nutrition: what we eat, drink, and breathe in our daily life.

The *Soul* of the Human Temple is our consciousness, composed of "subtle bodies" and their faculties (expressing through the Psychospiritual Centers) which we feed through our desires, emotions, thoughts, aspirations, words and deeds that provide *meaning* and *purpose* in our lives. Specifically:

> Our *Will* is nourished by our *actions* and *movement*;
> Our *Heart* is nourished by our *feelings* and *warmth*;
> Our *Mind* is nourished by our *thoughts* and *light*.

The *Spirit* of the Human Temple is our Divine Spark which awakens by the free expression of Its Energies: Light, Fire, and Life in our consciousness and physical body.

B. The construction and use of one's own personal "home" Temple and Sanctuary.

When beginning serious and regular personal transformation and psychospiritual work leading to an expanded consciousness, higher and more refined energies, and spiritual Awakening (and especially when following the work outlined in the Llewellyn Spiritual Sciences Series and described in this Handbook) it is highly recommended that the Candidate build his or her own Temple and Sanctuary in his or her *home* and *imagination,* each being as much as possible an *exact replica* of the other!

Here are some basic guidelines and a suggested blue-print for such an endeavor:

1. A special place should be dedicated, purified, and consecrated for worship, psychospiritual exercises, and the expansion of consciousness. This can range from setting up an actual Chapel with an Altar in a special room to setting up a special spot in one's bed or armchair which will be dedicated to such purposes. The middle course would be to set up a Sanctuary or Altar in one's bedroom or guest room for such purposes.

2. A special time each day and each week should be selected for temple work and worship. For a variety of psychological, psychic, and spiritual reasons, it is very important that a specific time be established and used regularly! This could be in the morning upon waking up, at noon, in the evening before going to sleep, or at sunrise or sunset. Once set, it should be adhered to as much as possible.

3. As this aspect of the Work is essentially a *personal one,* it is important that the Temple be properly "guarded" against strangers or people who are not very close friends and involved with the Work. Perhaps one's Mate, a spiritual Brother or Sister, or one's Guide if there is one, could be invited to cleanse and consecrate the Temple and to participate occasionally in the Work that is being done there. This is a very important rule to follow to create a certain "psychospiritual atmosphere" and to preserve certain energies and vibration.

4. This Temple and Sanctuary should consist of the following essentials in the physical world which

are then recreated and activated in the Candidate's *imagination:*

a. Symbols, locations, and objects representing the Human Aura and the Various "subtle bodies" (etheric, astral, mental and spiritual).

b. Symbols, locations and objects representing the Tree of Life and its basic Psychospiritual Centers in the Three Pillars of *Form, Consciousness,* and *Force* (in the human anatomy, the Pillar of Form is on the Right while the Pillar of Force is on the Left, while in the Temple it is the other way around. The Pillar of Consciousness is always in the Middle, representing the Middle Pillar).

c. The Four Cardinal Points, Archangels, and Elements should also be organized with appropriate symbols, locations and objects.

d. The Colors of the Spectrum of visible light with related astrological, qabalistic, and alchemical symbols should be properly designated in their appropriate place.

e. The Seven Functions of the Psyche with their associated psychospiritual Processes could also be included and appropriately symbolized and designated: Willing and Concentration, Thinking and Meditation, Feeling and Devotion, Imagination and Visualization, Intuition and Invocation-Evocation, Biopsychic Drives and Energy Transformation, and Sensations with Inner Observation. Here, one could also include the four basic stages of the Great Work:

Concentration, Meditation, Contemplation, and Theurgic Work.

f. Angelic Presences and Higher Spiritual
Beings should have their appropriate
place, symbols, and representations.

g. Finally, there should be a *central flame*, a
Candle or a set of Candles, representing
the Spiritual Energies in their Trinitary
expression of *light, fire* and *life*.

5. An Altar should be set up representing the Heart
Center in the Eastern front of the Space dedicated
as the Temple. Behind it, one can put a Cross with
an Icon of the Christ above it, on either side of it
there could be two Icons representing the Male
and Female Angels of the Sanctuary working in
polarity to transform spiritual Energies. (if one
wishes to have other Icons representing the Virgin
Mary, Saints, or other Angelic Power, these can
also be set up). On the Altar, there should be a Red
or Pink Candle burning, representing the activated
Heart Center. Also, one can put the Bible or the
Ritual Book one is using there. Chairs at specific
locations could be set up to represent the various
Centers, and in particular, the Center from which
the Candidate is working as the Officiant or Priest.
Finally, a variety of colors, astrological, qabalistic,
and alchemical symbols could be set up in their
appropriate places.

6. Specific Intentions, goals, or objectives should be
defined and affirmed, and the Temple and Sanctuary organized accordingly. For example: working
for healing, enlightenment, inspiration, the opening of the Intuition or the Heart Center or work on
the Seven Fundamentals as described in this
Handbook. These may have a duration of a day, a

week, one month, or even one year.

7. Once the Temple and Sanctuary have been defined, constructed, and consecrated in the physical world, it is then imperative that the Candidate produce, as accurately as possible, this temple, in his own *consciousness* and *imagination*, for it is there that the real work will be done, either directly or indirectly. Once the inner Temple and Sanctuary have been properly formulated activated, and crystallized in the consciousness of the Candidate, the latter may then transport the temple at will, and invoke it wherever he may be, in a physical Church, the Circle of Light Generator, in the office, at work, in a subway or car, in the street or somewhere in nature.

C. **The proper understanding and use of an established Temple or Church of one's Religion.**

We would strongly urge Candidates engaged in personal psychospiritual transformation to attend regularly their own Church or Temple and to participate consciously and actively in its Worship Services. There are three basic reasons for this:

1. The Candidate can thereby participate in a collective effort and in a type of Service which is not available to him in his own personal Temple, or in that of an esoteric group (and here, we are thinking specifically of the Catholic and Orthodox Liturgies and the Eucharist) to which he can and should bring all the training, "tools," and results of his own personal work.

2. When the particular prayer covered by one of our "Seven Fundamentals" is sung or recited in the public Temple, the Candidate should use it theurgically, bringing to his mind and evoking in his

consciousness all of the materials, energies, correspondences, and practical applications he has succeeded in discovering and experiencing through his own personal meditation and work. This process would then act as a "review exam" and as an effective preparation for consciously and actively participating in the Eucharist, the attunement of, and communication between, the human and the spiritual Self.

3. The Candidate can also perform a genuine and effective Service for the other participants and the officiating Priest by personally linking his Superconscious with the conscious, and by making the symbols, prayers, and rituals that are being used "come alive" in his consciousness, generating an outpouring and downpouring of the Divine Light, Fire, and Life in his own Aura and through his Tree of Life. By the law of *resonance* this will enable the other participants and the Officiating Priest, who have and are expressing Faith though not necessarily the esoteric knowledge, to make these symbols, prayers, and rituals also come alive for them and to speak to them thus greatly enriching and enlivening the value and function of the Liturgy.

In the outer Church or Temple, the Candidate can also *see* and *project the meanings, correspondences, and applications* of his own personal living Temple, his Psyche and Consciousness, and of his personal home Temple.

The Candidate can also recreate this Temple in his own imagination by the simultaneous use of Concentration, Meditation, Devotion, and Visualization, and use it as a "telesmatic image" or Magical Image—as a transformer of Consciousness and Energy to contact the Greater Temple and Sanctuary in the Inner Planes.

If we take a large and heterogeneous group and combine it with the old Liturgies, the psychospiritual atmosphere of the church, and with the inevitable "attendance" of this religious Service by Spiritual Beings on the "Other Side," we shall find that this Service becomes very alive and beneficial for all participants and for the community at large.

D. The proper understanding and use of a Temple of esoteric group or a spiritual Brotherhood.

The same fundamental principles and core insights that we applied to the Inner Living Temple, to the Personal Home Temple, and to the Temple of one's religion can also be applied to the construction, understanding, and utilization of the Temple and Rituals of an esoteric group. The only basic difference will be that here the Temple and the Rituals will be formulated and utilized for a specific purpose by a group of trained persons whose central aim is to consciously experience and live the Rituals they are using. It is at this point that the basic training that the Candidate received in understanding and using Symbols and Rituals will prove invaluable and is, generally, *required* of their members by all *genuine* and *effectively* functioning esoteric organizations. Thus, the Candidate will be expected to know about, and be able to formulate his or her various Auras, Tree of Life and their psychospiritual Centers; to know about and be able to work with the 7 Functions of the Psyche and their related psychospiritual processes; to be able to work with, decode, and make the Symbols and Rituals come alive, unveil their mysteries, and operate as Energy and Consciousness transformers; to know and be able to construct and work with an operational inner and outer Temple and Sanctuary; to know and be able to work with Concentration, Meditation, Contemplation, and

Theurgy; and finally, to be able to invoke, draw down, and circulate the Divine Light, Fire, and Life of the Divine Spark. In essence, the whole preparatory work or genuine "Neophyte's Degree" consists in outlining the knowledge and doing the practical psychospiritual exercises we have been describing in this Handbook, or their functional equivalents.

Thus, it is at this point or "level" that the true work and purpose of this Handbook can best be realized ... when the Candidate will himself or herself become an initiate of a valid esoteric order, or a priest or priestess of a living religion!

5
THE SEVEN FUNDAMENTALS AND THE PRIMORDIAL TRADITION

In all the World Religions and great Philosophical Traditions a major separation has always been drawn between two distinct aspects of human reality: the Sacred and the Profane.

The Sacred generally referred to religious activity where God was supposed to be present and where the participants were supposed to be aware of the Presence of God; whereas the Profane generally referred to mundane and economic activity where God was supposed to be absent and where the participants were supposed to be unaware of the Divine Presence.

Actually, this had very little to do with God and with the world, but everything to do with the *state of consciousness* of the participants.

In its Sacred mode, the consciousness of the participants was expanded and exalted so as to make them aware of the three-fold aspect of reality: Physical, Human, and Spiritual, while in its Profane mode, the consciousness of the participants was restricted and focused only upon the physical, and at times, the human dimension of reality.

Likewise, all religions were also subdivided into two fundamental aspects: the *Exoteric* and the *Esoteric*. The Exoteric aspect of religion was given only to the masses who functioned in a three-fold mode of consciousness: the sensate, the emotional, and the mental, and who basically received the "letter" of the Mysteries and their intellectual explanation.

On the other hand, the Esoteric aspect of religion was given to the Few who had awakened their fourth level of consciousness—*Spiritual Consciousness*.

One of the most fundamental differences between these two basic aspects is the basic conception of God that was conveyed. In its Exoteric mode, God was personified, anthropomorphized, and located in the world; here Salvation was to be obtained by conforming to the dogmas and rules of the organized Church and to be achieved *after one's death!*

In its Esoteric mode, God was to be experienced as *light* manifesting as Consciousness, Love, and Creative Energy, and was found to be located in the Being and Consciousness of the Candidate himself! Esoterically, Salvation was achieved by actualizing one's potential and developing one's faculties: thinking, feeling and willing in particular, so as to become a coordinated vehicle or "Temple" for God's Spirit to manifest in the world as *Divine Wisdom, Divine Love,* and *Divine Will.*

The *body* and the *letter* of the Mysteries were passed on and given to the people through the Exoteric aspect, but its living Soul and Spirit could only be personally achieved and experienced through its Esoteric manifestation.

The fundamental principle ever to keep in mind here, especially when reflecting upon the many religions and the One Universal Religion, is that one's conception of God, of the Ultimate Reality, and of oneself, is always and unavoidably a Function of One's Level of Consciousness which therefore changes, grows, and unfolds with the expansion and transformation of one's consciousness!

The truly revealed and universal aspect of the Symbols, Myths, and Rituals of the Great Religions is precisely that they are valid and living for all human beings, on *all* levels of consciousness and being; but, keep in mind that they are *not* all the same, they are ever transforming themselves so as to either veil or unveil certain basic truths and universal principles. In other words, they demand an *active* participation on the part of the candidate who will receive from them in direct proportion to what he or she puts into them, or "brings" to them . . .

Practical work for this chapter:

1. Go to your chosen "Temple" (whether it's an Inner Temple in your Imagination or a location in the physical world). Find a relaxed position, turn to the East and look at, or formulate, your Sanctuary, form your outer or inner Circle and begin the preparatory work:

2. Close your eyes and go through the basic steps of:

   > **Introversion:** refocus your attention and energies from the outside/physical world to the inner/psychological world.

   > **Supraversion:** raise your center of consciousness by focusing your *attention,* your *thoughts,* and your *desires* and *love* upon the Head Psychospiritual Center.

   > **Make Contact:** get in touch with, and experience the Light, Warmth, and Power that emanate from the "Sun" that overshadows your Head.

Infraversion: bring down into your *heart* Psychospiritual Center the Light, Fire and Life you have contacted in your Head Center.

Center and Align Yourself: by feeling and experiencing the Energies and Power of the Light filling your whole being and transforming your consciousness.

Radiate and Circulate the Light and Energies: through all your Psychospiritual Centers, coming down the Left Side to the Feet Center and returning on the Right Side, then coming down the Middle Pillar in front to return on your back to the Head Center from the Feet Center.

3. Visualize your Aura or Alembic, formulate the Tree of Life with all of its Centers ... then focus all your attention and gaze upon your Sanctuary, residing in the Heart Psychospiritual Center. Mentally and visually *enter it* ...

4. The specific intention or focus for this chapter is to Meditate upon and reach your own insights and conclusions concerning the following subjects:

Yourself: Who and what are you?

Why have you come to Earth?

What are the central purpose and the basic lessons of the present life?

God: Who and What is God?

What is your relationship to God at present?

How can you improve and make this relationship "come alive"?

Religion: What is religion to you at this point?

Does the distinction between the Exoteric

and the Esoteric Aspects of religion mean anything to you at this point? Can they help reconcile the religion you were born into and your spiritual aspirations, and if so, how?

Seven Fundamentals: What is your present understanding and use, if any, of what we have called the Seven Fundamentals, namely:

1. Divine Names
2. Sign of the Cross
3. Lord's Prayer
4. Nicene Creed
5. Beatitudes
6. Ten Commandments
7. Hail Mary

5. If you are so inclined, you may attempt to contemplate these 10 basic topics, one by one, changing your state of consciousness and *becoming at one* with them to see what, if anything, will be revealed to you about them.

6. Finally, return to your normal state of consciousness, leave your Sanctuary, and write in your workbook what you have done and what is your present knowledge, understanding, and your past experience of these 10 basic topics. Once a year (on the anniversary date of when you began this work) you could go through the same procedure to see what changes and growth have occurred in the time that has elapsed.

7. If you are beginning on your Path of Personal Transformation and Spiritual Growth at this point, you might add, when you are still under the rubric of *Yourself*, the basic goals and objectives that you have for yourself for the coming year, and then to

meditate upon them, to add or delete from these goals, and finally write them down in your workbook . . . to check at the end of the year what you have, indeed, accomplished and what you have failed to accomplish.

There is another, more generic, set of 7 principles that could very profitably be meditated upon and incorporated into the daily life of the Candidate who is seeking to learn and master "The Nature and Use of Ritual for Spiritual Attainment."

These are the 7 great laws or dimensions that pertain to the holistic and preventive medicine of the future which are designed to ensure the optimum functioning of the body and the Psyche of the Candidate so that he has available at all times the maximum amount of energy or vitality, mental clarity, emotional centeredness, and control over his various "consciousness vehicles" and their "organs" and "functions."

These 7 great laws or dimensions are:

1. **Nutrition:** eating the right *quantity* and *quality* of food, and with the proper mixing of them for one's age, personality type, and life style.

2. **Sleep:** getting the right amount of sleep, which means not too much or too little sleep every day, and of course, good quality sleep.

3. **Physical Exercise:** making sure that one strengthens one's body through exercise, sports, or other physical activities.

4. **Sexual and Love Life:** getting not too much or too little sex, and especially, good quality sex, or *transmuting* the sexual energies if a suitable partner is unavailable. This is a dimension which is still very

much misunderstood and greatly abused at the present time, sexual education notwithstanding!

5. Social Life: monitoring and controlling the quantity and quality of one's relationships with significant others, the basic composition of one's psychosocial network, and the energies and cultural materials which are exchanged in one's human relationships.

6. Spiritual Life: getting in touch regularly with one's Higher Self and with the Ultimate Reality to balance, harmonize, and vivify one's entire being and life. Paradoxically, this dimension, which is the kingpin of the whole structure of holistic and preventive medicine, is often either neglected, identified with the emotional and mental life, or with the psychosocial and sociocultural dimensions . . . and the last one to be properly recognized and fully developed!

These basic principles could be meditated upon by the Candidate, incorporated into his workbook, so that the progress (the degree to which the Candidate can incorporate them progressively into his or her life and *live them*) that is being made can be monitored.

6
DIVINE NAMES

Their Nature and Use

The Sacred Traditions of the Past have always assigned a great deal of importance to Names: the Names of God, the Names of Spiritual Powers, the Names of human beings, or plants, animals, or minerals.

Many Spiritual Traditions of both the East and the West have established specialized disciplines dealing primarily with the repetition and vibrations of Names of Power. For example:

Mantra Yoga
Japa Yoga
Theurgy
Activation of the Tree of Life
The Way of the Name
Numerology

The modern social sciences are also slowly but surely recognizing the psychosocial importance of Names, as witnessed by the "Labeling theory." Finally, the entire history of Science, both natural and social, and eventually also Spiritual, consists of and can be measured by the creation of new concepts.

What then is a Name; what does it contain and what

functions does it fulfill?

Names are symbols and psychic media which convey and elicit the various units of human consciousness we call intuitions, thoughts, feelings, and vital energies. As such, Names are the true units of human consciousness, acting as streams of focused thoughts, emotions and "bundles of energy." They are the mental lenses that focus our whole attention upon one aspect of reality, one power, or one being. Names also function as catalysts to awaken, invoke and evoke certain energies and states of consciousness in our Psyche. **In short, they are the psychospiritual means at our disposal to invoke a certain Presence and induce a certain state of consciousness by focusing our awareness.** Names are the intellectual tools by which we can recreate in ourselves an image or a facsimile of that which is without, or below, or above our consciousness and by which human beings create an inner psychospiritual cosmos. A Name contains the essence of that which it represents and its distinguishing characteristics (vibrations, frequencies, and materials) by which we can bring into consciousness that which lies in our subconscious, our unconscious, or our superconscious concerning these characteristics.

Esoterically speaking a Name is the means by which we can *know* something, by becoming its temporary channel and by recreating it or allowing it to express in our consciousness and in our being. This is why it is said in Genesis that human beings should name all the creatures of the air, sea and Earth, and all objects of Creation, and why the knowledge of the Names of God are so important: because human consciousness has to unfold and expand gradually to encompass all dimensions of being.

Finally, a Name is also a seed which we plant in the garden of our consciousness, feed with our attention, emotions, and thoughts, to enable it to grow and unfold therein. For it is a well-known fact that the mind takes on the form of the object it beholds and that the vital energies of the psyche run along the lines traced by the mind, bringing into consciousness and energizing that which we think about. A Word of Power is thus an ideal containing various energies and materials (intuitions, thoughts, feelings, and vital energies) which are crystallized and concretized, projected by the will, the mind, and the imagination (or the emotions, desires, and biopsychic drives) and then introjected in the Psyche so that temporarily the operator can identify with it and become the channel to manifest its attributes in the world.

A Name contains a certain *sound* (vibrations and frequencies), certain *traits and attributes* (ideas and intuitions), and certain *images and colors* (emotions and energies) which we can activate and recreate in ourselves.

As such, there is a true "science of Names" and a "practical art of Names" which the Candidate must learn and master in order to make progress on the Path. Let us take four basic examples: the first example in nature, the second in human relations, the third in spiritual aspirations, and the fourth in one of the Names of God.

When we utter the Name "cell" we direct our attention to the smallest unit of biological life: a unit of protoplasm with a nucleus and an enclosing membrane. Whatever we have observed, learned or experienced concerning a biological cell will then emerge in our field of consciousness and whatever we may yet observe, learn, or experience will add to our store of knowledge which makes this an open, ongoing, growing process. Normally, we do not attach or evoke emotions pertaining to a cell but we may link various associations and correspondences to it that may trigger and activate our intuition.

In human relations, there are a number of Names of Power that we could use; they only have to be the Name of a person we know, love and look up to, which could be our mother, father, brother, sister, girl friend or boy friend, or even a teacher. The moment we utter the generic or specific Name (e.g. Mother or Alice) we evoke in our imagination the appearance or face of that person, and his/her basic attributes, what he/she represents to us, and what happens to us when we are with him/her. The Name will act as a lens to direct, at least momentarily, all of our thoughts, all of our feelings, and our whole attentions upon that person who will thus draw attention and energy away from other foci and recreate the Being and Presence of that person within ourselves! At that point that recreated person will be with us and in us and will have a powerful effect upon our emotions in particular, and our state of consciousness in general. This Name will act as a powerful *consciousness* and *energy transformer*. The power and effectiveness of this transformer will obviously depend upon two fundamental variables:

1. How we perceive and feel towards that person—upon our state of consciousness—which is the intrapsychic dimension.

2. What we have lived through and experienced with that person: the sum total of what we shared mentally, emotionally, and existentially with that person—which is the interpsychic dimension. This aspect is open ended in the future so that we may well nourish and expand this relationship, adding to it or chiseling away some of its aspects, and thereby change it.

The same dynamic applies to the use of any Name on any level of Being and can serve as a good model and source of inspiration as to how to "use" Names of Power of certain virtues, qualities, or Beings as well as Divine Names which, as the Names of God, represent our highest aspirations and points of contact with Reality.

Whether we are using the Name of an object of Nature, of a human being, of an abstract quality or virtue, of an Angel, Archangel, Spiritual Power, or of God, the basic process and preparation are the same. The "body" of the Name, its alphabetical spelling and sound, must be planted in our garden of consciousness. There it must be fed, nourished, and cultivated so that it can grow and unfold within our being, unveiling its soul (or sets of meanings and correspondences) and eventually bringing us in contact with its Spirit, the Life and Reality to which it corresponds.

Specifically this means:

a. To focus all your attention upon the Name—to *concentrate* on it.

b. To decipher and reflect upon its hidden meanings and message—to *meditate* regularly on it.

c. To open our heart to it and pour all our feelings into it—to express *devotion* for it.

d. To allow it to manifest in different images or symbols that reveal its nature and function for us at that time—to *visualize* it.

e. To empty our minds and make space in our consciousness and dedicate time to it so that its higher meanings, correspondences, and mysteries might gradually be revealed to us as we use it in Invocation/Evocation.

This whole process should be carried out at regular intervals, forming the basis of a Meditation upon it (to the extent that we are able to do so). Altering our state of consciousness, we should then Contemplate the Name, entering into it and becoming at one with it so that the Divine Spark in us might gradually reveal and manifest its Spiritual Mysteries to us.

According to the meaning and associations that a given

Word of Power or Divine Name might have for a given Candidate, and according to his own state of consciousness and level of being, it might take from weeks to months or even years to make any Name become truly "hot," "operational," and "alive" for him. By this we mean to make it act experientially and effectively as the energy and consciousness transformer it is designed to be.

Then, and only then, as we "vibrate" the Name or "intone" it, will it bring to consciousness all the thoughts, ideas and correspondences, all the feelings and emotions, all the images and symbols, all the intuitions and inspirations, and all the energies and vibrations that we have charged it with and endowed it with over its long process of "cultivation."

In a flash, all our knowledge and experiences connected with the Name will be evoked in our consciousness, eliciting in turn all the vibrations, energies, and materials to which they correspond. Eventually, we will actually become the *channel* or the three-fold Temple (in the physical, astral and mental worlds) to manifest its Spirit and Essence—to Live and Radiate its Attributes.

Lastly, let the Candidate bear in mind that he may use any well-established Name of Power of the Sacred Traditions—whether they be on the Occult, Mystical or Magical Paths, of the ancient or modern Religions, or he may even devise his own Name of Power to be used either by himself or in his group. However, here there is an important difference: if the Candidate uses a well-known and time-hallowed Name of Power he will eventually contact its Group-Soul, or Egregor, and have a great reservoir of energy, meanings and corespondences at his disposal which have been built up by the individuals and groups who have used it over time, thus contacting the collective Unconscious. Whereas if he makes up his own Name of Power, this aspect and these reservoirs and contacts will be lacking!

Proposed Practical Work for this Chapter:
1. Choose the Name of an object of nature and turn it into a Name of Power, using the aforementioned methodology. For the sake of illustration, let us take the Sun.

     (We recommend using common sense above all else). Go and look at the Sun on a cloudless and clear day. *Don't stare at it!* Look at the Sun at sunrise, at noon, and then finally at sunset and impress upon your consciousness its image, characteristics, and impact upon your state of consciousness.

     Read and reflect about the Sun in different scientific, philosophical, and religious works, distilling the knowledge that human beings have derived from it and make a synthesis of it in your own mind.

     Now begin the esoteric work in earnest: concentrate all your attention upon the Sun, direct all your thoughts upon the Sun and evoke the synthesis of your knowledge of the Sun at this point, then open your heart to the Sun and observe what desires, feelings, emotions and aspirations the Sun stirs up in your being. Invoke one or more images of the Sun and visualize them clearly on the screen of your imagination. Finally, make room in your consciousness for the Sun and watch for the intuitions it might activate in you. This is a structured Meditation upon the Sun.

     Continue by altering your state of consciousness and attempting to Contemplate the Sun in your consciousness: invoke it . . . open your mind,

heart, and will to it . . . ask questions about the Sun
concerning its nature, function, and role in your
life, and then watch for any answers, for any new
energies, desires, feelings, thoughts, and inspirations that might descend upon your consciousness.

Decide at what times and set of conditions,
inner and outer, you might want to invoke the Sun
in your consciousness, and for what purposes.
Then actually do it! Invoke the Sun in specific
situations and states of mind and discover what its
Name and its invocation can actually do for you,
what changes and transformations it will bring
about. You might want to use the Consciousness
Checklist (see Appendix) before and after as a
monitoring device.

Finally, record in your workbook what you
have done, when, where, and with what results.
Keep an accurate description of your inner and
outer life in your diary to catch some subtle and
preconscious influences and tranformations this
work may bring about. Thus, learn about the nature
and use of Names of Power taking your own consciousness, being, and life as its main "laboratory"
and your own experiences as its final "measuring
rod."

In my own meditations and experiences, I have come
to the conclusion that the Sun is a trinity emanating physical Light, Warmth, and Life; that this trinity at the human
level corresponds to Knowledge, Love, and Creative Energy
as it is refracted through our Head, Heart, and Will, manifesting as the 7 colors of the spectrum: red, orange, yellow,
green, blue, indigo, and violet which represent, in human
consciousness, and impact and affect the 7 functions of
the psyche:

Willing (red)
Thinking (yellow)
Feeling (green)
Imagination (blue)
Intuition (violet)
Biopsychic Drives (orange)
Sensations (indigo)

The Sun has taught me that:

a. If I want to become more luminous I must give of myself becoming more selfless;

b. If I am confused, emotionally depressed, or drained of energy, I can bring the Spiritual Energies of the Inner Sun to light up my consciousness, to warm my heart, and to vivify my will.

Next, we can choose the name of an important person and turn it into a Name of Power, using the same methodology. For the sake of illustration, take the Name of a person you know well and admire as an ideal model.

Go and spend some time with that person. Observe how that person thinks, feels, makes decisions, speaks, and acts; how that person relates to others and how that person copes with certain problems and situations in life. Using the Consciousness checklist, study the impact that this person has upon you when you are in his/her presence and how it affects your consciousness and behavior.

Now make the connection between the person himself/herself and his/her Name, just as a picture is connected to the object it represents. Then reflect upon the essential qualities and traits of that person: what constitutes the *essence* of that person for you at this point in time.

Begin the esoteric work in earnest! Concentrate all your attention upon that person, direct all your thoughts upon that person and evoke the synthesis of your knowledge and experience of that person at this point. Then, open your heart to that person and observe what desires, feelings, emotions, and aspirations that person stirs in your being. Invoke an image or symbol of that person and visualize it clearly on the screen of your imagination.

Finally, make room in your consciousness for that person and watch for what intuitions the chosen symbol of that person might activate in you. This is your structured Meditation upon that person.

Continue by altering your state of consciousness and attempting to Contemplate that person: invoke the Name of that person . . . open your mind, heart, and will to that person . . . become one with that person absorbing and integrating the qualities of that person you would like to awaken and activate in your life . . . and then watch what happens in them and what happens in you. Decide at what times and in what circumstances, inner and outer, you might want to "invoke that person" in your consciousness, and for what purposes.

Then, *actually do it!* Invoke the Name of that person in specific situations and states of mind, and discover what this Name and its invocation can do for you, what changes and transformations it will bring about in your inner and outer worlds, in consciousness and behavior. Use the Consciousness Checklist before and after as a monitoring device.

Finally, record in your workbook what you have done, when, where, and with what results. Keep an accurate description of your outer and inner life in your diary to catch the subtle and preconscious influences and transformations this work may bring about. In this fashion, continue to learn about the nature and use of Names of Power.

Let me give you an example of how I have used (and still use) the Name of one of my teachers, who is an 85 year-old woman still alive in Paris, and whom I have known and been inspired by for over 25 years. To me, she represents the highest incarnation of a spiritually awakened Woman I have been privileged to encounter in this world, and beyond that, of the Feminine Principle as well as Human Nature at its best!

In her presence, I have become transformed: being more myself in its higher sense, more alive, more creative, generous, and functioning at a higher level of consciousness. When I invoke her Name (alone, in a group setting, or in a ritual setting) I immediately feel her presence there and no longer feel alone, but instead connected to God, to Humanity, and to Nature. All that I know about and have experienced with her immediately returns to me and is present with me as her Spirit is connected with mine, and I become transformed again with powerful motivations and urges to become the better person I can be. I have used her Name for a variety of purposes in a variety of settings: when I had felt alone or depressed; when my creativity was blocked or when I have let myself fall prey to lower states of consciousness; when I need to be more courageous, more objective, or selfless; and when I wanted to contact certain energies, vibrations and psychospiritual materials or Beings that could help me, or the group I was doing spiritual work with.

Thus, she provided me with a functional Ideal Model and her Name was the means by which her Spirit could come in contact with me and work through me while enabling me to develop and unfold, little by little, the same qualities and faculties she already possesses.

2. Choose the Name of a Spiritual Ideal, Power or Being and turn it into your own personal Name of Power, using the same methodology and steps.

For the sake of illustration, let me tell you what the Name of Pallas Athena, the Greek Goddess of Wisdom and Courage, has meant to me and how, over the years, I have transformed it and used it as a Name of Power.

When I was very, very young I used to behold with the eyes of my imagination a very beautiful, inspiring and luminous woman clad in a blue robe and holding a red sword and shield. I would have long discussions with her, what we today would call an inner dialogue, and she would tell me many things and take me on many adventures.

When I began to read Greek mythology, I immediately identified her as Pallas Athena, the Greek goddess of Wisdom and War. At that point, I read all I could about her and spent long hours beholding her, dressed in different ways, and involved in different activities.

Unconsciously, perhaps, I focused all my attention, all my thoughts and projected all my feelings and aspirations unto her and slowly formulated my favorite image or representation of her and in which she would appear to me when I would invoke and vibrate her Name: Athena.

Later, I even went to Greece and searched for various Temples dedicated to her and looked for her statues and for legends of her heroic deeds.

When I felt fearful or discouraged, or would be about to give up on a difficult or dangerous (but worthwhile) endeavor I would call upon her Name and she would appear to me in my imagination: then I would feel her merging with me, becoming at one with me and infusing me with new courage, new inspiration, new life, and the determination to carry through my endeavor.

When I felt alone or unbalanced, I used the same process with the same results and was immediately inwardly transformed and taken upon a different level of consciousness where the same mundane events and circumstances would then appear quite different than they had just a few moments before.

As She manifested to me, and manifested some of Her Attributes through me, I felt lifted up to Her Plane of Being and could, momentarily think with Her Mind, feel with Her Heart, choose what She wanted and see with Her Eyes and so in this way I became another, better aspect of myself.

Eventually, it became such that just by vibrating Her Name or invoking Her Presence would be enough to bring about a profound consciousness-transformation in my being that would alter my behavior.

3. Choose a Divine Name representing the highest Ideal you can aspire to and conceive of at that point, and turn it into your personal Name of Power using that same methodology and steps.

Let us use the Name of Jesus Christ, which for the Christian Mystic is the highest of all Names of Power and the "Name before which all Heavenly Powers bow." Exoterically, Jesus of Nazareth, Who at the age of 30 became the Christ, represents the Second Person of the Trinity Who came to Earth so that humans could find their way back to God and become at one with God. As the Orthodox Church puts it:

"God became Man, so that Man could become God."

Esoterically speaking Jesus was the first human who fully identified the human self with the Spiritual Self, so that the Divine Spark could now consciously incarnate on Earth and act therein.

Vibrationally, His Name is connected with the Divine Essence, with the Divine Spark, so that when used with the faith and when the Candidate is ready He too might temporarily become a Christ, a Temple for the living God. By vibrating and invoking His Name, He comes down to us so as to lift us up to Him, to Divinity.

Practical Work with this Process:

a.   Go to a Christian Church where an older Liturgy is being celebrated (Roman Catholic, Orthodox, Episcopalian, Liberal or old Catholic Mass) and participate in it, paying particular attention to what is said about Jesus Christ and done in His Name. See what happens to your consciousness using the Consciousness Checklist. Store in your memory what is said about and done in the Name of Jesus Christ.

b.   Read and reflect about Jesus Christ in the Christian Gospels and the Catechisms of older Churches (Catholic and Orthodox). Distill the knowledge you can gather there and make a synthesis of it in your own mind.

c.   Now begin the esoteric work in earnest: concentrate all your attention upon the Person, Life and Teachings of Jesus Christ, direct all your thoughts upon Jesus Christ and evoke the synthesis of your knowledge of Him at this point. Then open your heart to Him and observe what desires, feelings, emotions and aspirations stir up in your being. Invoke His Image and visualize it clearly upon the screen of your imagination. Finally make room in your consciousness for Him and watch for what intuitions and revelations might come to you. This is your structured Meditation upon that Being.

d.   Bear in mind that Christ is in you, that He is your Divine Spark! Alter your state of consciousness and seek to Contemplate Him. Invoke His Name, open your mind, heart, and will to Him, and become one with Him, absorbing and integrating His Being and Qualities, so that He may manifest through your consciousness and being and that you may become Him, at least temporarily . . . and watch for what happens to you at this point.

e.   Decide at what times and in what circumstances, inner and outer, you might want to invoke His Name in your consciousness and for what purposes.

f.   Then, *actually do it:* invoke the Name of Jesus Christ in specific situations and states of consciousness, and discover what His Name and Its invocation can do for you, and for the functioning of your mind, your heart, and your will.

g.   Finally, record in your workbook what you have done, when, where, and with what results. Keep an accurate description of your outer and inner life in your diary to catch the subtle and preconscious influences and transformations this work may bring about.

You might want to use the same procedure and steps to construct and unfold your own personal Name of Power. Make sure to focus upon the ideal and its basic characteristics that you want to become and incarnate as you weave them into this Name of Power.

Use this Name of Power that you have created for several weeks or even months without mentioning it to anyone or telling anyone what you are doing. In other words, learn to keep silent so as not to diffuse your concentration and energies and not to bring foreign influences to bear upon your Aura, Tree of Life, and Work . . . at least until you achieve some of the desired results.

7
THE SIGN OF THE CROSS

Its Nature and Use

Only when the candidate has mastered the science and art of using Divine Names and Words of Power, when they have become "alive" and "consciousness and energy-stirring" within his being, is he truly ready for the next step in his spiritual awakening, and that next step is to *understand* and *use* the Sign of the Cross.

If the candidate does not have operational Names of Power, which evoke the Light, Fire and Life into his consciousness, then he is not ready for this next Step. He must know how to "vibrate" and "entone" a Name of Power physically (or outwardly) and psychologically (or inwardly) so that each word will immediately and noticeably affect his consciousness, awaken his Higher Energies and Vibrations (and the Power to which they correspond) so that their Soul and Spirit will penetrate in his being, dwell in his consciousness and lift him up to their Plane . . . then, and only then, will the Sign of the Cross become "alive" for him, to reveal Its Mysteries, and become what the Apostle Paul rightly called "the Power of God."

The essence of the Sign of the Cross is none other than the proper vibration of certain Names of Power in certain Psychospiritual Centers, awakening them, "lighting them up," and using their combined Energies and Powers.

Each of the individual Names of Power can be properly vibrated in their appropriate Psychospiritual Centers with the proper Concentration, Meditation, and Devotion, and the Candidate will have genuine results but it would not be the same as using the Names of Power in a synchronized fashion. For it is in their mutual interaction and combination, which creates a Psychospiritual Synthesis, that a whole greater than the sum of its parts can be obtained and enfleshed, i.e. the cleansing or purification of the Aura, the consecration of the Inner Temple, and the formulation of a "spiritual Blood System" can be established through which Grace (the Divine Light, Fire, and Life of the Higher Self) can flood the consciousness of the Candidate and lift this consciousness up into the "Spiritual Temple not made by human hands . . . " where the real Mysteries of Regeneration, Rebirth, and Spiritual Awakening will be Lived and made Manifest.

To work with the Ritual of the Cross, which involves different degrees and various traditions, we need the usual "tools" that we outlined and described in the first chapter of this book, namely:

I. To be able to visualize and experience one's own Aura or Alembic.

2. To be able to formulate, visualize, and experience one's own Tree of Life, and its Psychospiritual Centers.

3. To have the proper understanding and use of the 7 Functions of the Psyche with their related Psychospiritual Processes (which I have nicknamed the "muscles of consciousness.")

4. To have an understanding of and have begun the 4 fundamental stages of the work of Personal Transformation, Consciousness Expansion and Spiritual

Awakening.

In addition to these, which we now assume the Candidate is familiar with and is capable of using effectively, we also need to have planted in the Garden of our Consciousness and activated *three key Divine Names* (Father, Son, and Holy Spirit), 4 particular Psychospiritual Centers (Head, Heart, Left and Right Shoulder) and the ability to create various inner realities*, and to work with and be able to move around Light, Fire, and Life in our consciousness.

5. To have a working relationship with the Divine Names: *Father, Son, and Holy Spirit,* as we are going to work, for the purpose of illustration with the Catholic Christian Sign of the Cross.

6. To have a working knowledge of the Psychospiritual Centers; in particular the Head, the Heart, and the Shoulder Centers.

7. To have a vivid Imagination when using Guided Imagery, to become fully absorbed by and immersed in the inner visualizations we will be doing and which involves sensing, feeling, and experiencing Light, Fire, and Life, and to visualize moving these about in our Aura, thereby awakening, vivifying, and bringing into consciousness various energies, vibrations, and states of consciousness.

Thus, when we vibrate "In the Name of the *Father . . . "* we refer to the *Divine Wisdom* at the spiritual level, and the highest knowledge and state of consciousness we can evoke at the psychological level. This Divine Name is linked with the Head (Psychospiritual) Center and manifests Grace, or

---

*Using Guided Imagery

Spiritual Energy, as Light, which illumines the Inner Worlds as physical light, illumines the physical world, and which enables us to see and to become aware of and to orient ourselves in the material world . . .

When we vibrate the Divine Name "of the *Son* . . . " we refer to *Divine Love* at the spiritual level, and the highest capacity to love and to feel we can evoke at the psychological level. This Divine Name is linked with the Heart (Psychospiritual) Center and manifests Grace or spiritual Energy as *Fire*, which enables us to feel and to experience joy in ourselves and in the world—which brings taste and a special quintessence to whatever we become aware of: the experience of Love and Loving.

Finally, when we vibrate the Divine Name "of the *Holy Spirit* . . . " we refer to the *Divine Creative Energies* at the spiritual level, and the highest vitality and life-giving energy we can evoke at the psychological level. This Divine Name is linked with the Left and Right shoulder (Psychospiritual) Centers, the Right Shoulder being the masculine aspect, with the Left Shoulder being the feminine one. This Divine Name manifests Grace, or Spiritual Energy, as *Life* which awakens, vivifies, and brings to life all the inner dimensions and powers—which is the true, operational meaning of the "power of the Holy Spirit."

When we look at the Sign of the Cross as a whole we are asked to direct our attention upon, to feel, visualize and invoke/evoke the various energies and materials related to the Names; and then to concentrate upon, medidate upon, and contemplate them using *Theurgically* each one of them until they become "alive" and operational in our consciousness.

From another perspective, the Head Psychospiritual Center can be visualized as a bright noonday sun, slightly above and larger than our physical head, yet interpenetrating it and glowing with white, yellow, and blue light. As we invoke the Name of the *Father,* this Center should become alive, hot, and activated, which means that we should be able to sense, feel, and experience its warmth, vibrations, and power as a slight tension, pressure, and inner stirrings and activities in that Center. This will immediately change and expand our consciousness, and bring new ideas and insights.

The Heart Psychospiritual Center can be visualized as a rising sun slightly deeper and greater than the physical heart and glowing with pink, orange, and yellow light. As we invoke the Name of the *Son,* this Center should also become alive, hot and activated which means that we should be able to sense, feel, and experience a great warmth, fullness and life permeating, suffusing, and emanating from this Center. The Heart Center should then become alive and stir up into activity, expanding as a balloon which is being blown up; this will immediately change and intensify our feelings and bring new emotions, and a sensation of joy and fullness into the Heart Center, which will then spread to envelop our whole being.

The Right Shoulder Center can be visualized as a setting sun slightly deeper and greater than the physical right shoulder, and glowing with three different hues of red light whereas the Left Shoulder Center can be visualized as a dazzling blue sun with varying shades of blue light glowing from it. As we invoke the Name of the *Holy Spirit,* these two Shoulder Centers should, likewise, become alive, hot, and activated which means that we sould be able to sense, feel, and experience an electric current or power permeating and emanating from these Centers. The Shoulder Centers should then become alive and pulsate with Life and Power. This will immediately change and amplify our will and energies, and bring new vitality and life into our whole

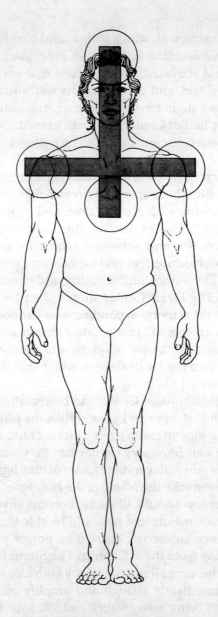

Catholic Sign of the Cross

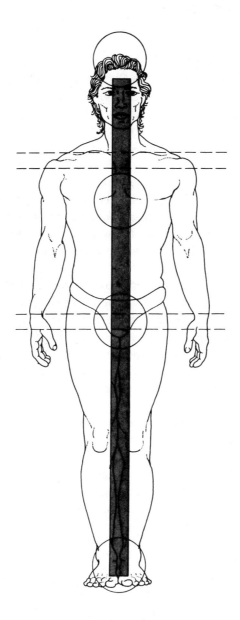

Advanced Sign of the Cross

being, and energize our whole consciousness.

The Catholic Christian Sign of the Cross is normally formulated and vibrated between the Head and the Heart Centers, on the vertical shaft, and between the Right and Left Shoulder Centers on the horizontal shaft, thus tracing and generating a Great Cross of Light in the aura of the Candidate which acts as a Light and Energy distributing system, or "nervous system" for his whole being.

In the more advanced form of the Sign of the Cross, it can be formulated and vibrated only on the vertical axis between the Head, Heart, and Genital Centers, and then extending down to the Feet Center, after crossing at the Hip or Shoulder Centers.

Diamonds or crystals of pure white Light can also be visualized rather than the various suns or spheres of multicolored Lights. There are technical or more advanced reasons for using either one or the other approach, but this is something that the Candidate must discover for himself. For the purposes of getting started and of illustration we will analyze only the first approach.

The white Head Psychospiritual Center is the normal home of the Divine Spark until it can descend and incarnate in the Heart. This Center is the great Reservoir or Source of all Energy, Life, and Consciousness and the central "switch" or "contact point" the candidate must activate for all subsequent work. It can be tapped and drawn upon to activate, alter, and expand consciousness and thinking through the energies of the Light as well as Will and Life at another vibratory level.

Generally it is visualized as a point of white Light expanding into a noonday sun of vibrating, pulsating, and radiating Sphere of Light and Power operating at the superconscious Level which can then transform and modulate

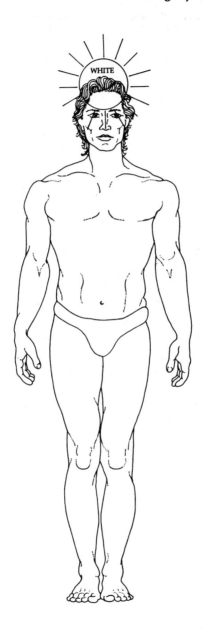

itself into yellow and blue according to the qualities it is approached with and drawn upon.

The major attributes associated with this Head Psychospiritual Center is *Divine Wisdom* which also implies Life and Will, without which there can be no Wisdom.

The pink Heart Psychospiritual Center is the normal home of the human ego . . . until the Spiritual Self can descend into it and fuse with it from the Head.

The Heart Psychospiritual Center is the great Reservoir and Source of all Love, Feelings, and Emotions, and the central transformer or prism for all the lights and Energies of the Psyche as well as the meeting point for the Soul and the Personality (the Higher and Lower Self).

The Heart Center can be tapped and drawn upon to awaken Love and Life and to transform consciousness, energies, and desires. Generally, it is visualized as a pink setting sun of vibrating, pulsating, and radiating Sphere of Light and Power operating at the conscious level which can transform and modulate itself into yellow and orange according to the qualities and virtues it is approached with and drawn upon.

The major attribute for the Heart Center is *Divine Love* and the free giving of oneself.

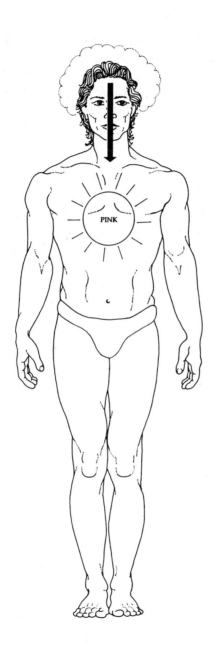

The red and blue Shoulder Psychospiritual Centers are the normal home of our vitality, nervous energy, and motivating force. These Centers are the great Reservoirs and Sources of human will, life force and action-energy which combine and fuse the Male and Female Polarities and energies which are vital for the marriage of the soul and the personality, and for the various actions we can take in the material world.

Generally, these Centers are visualized as Red and Blue Spheres of vibrating, pulsating, and vivifying energies which can suffuse the whole Aura of the Candidate with the color *purple* when they are properly balanced and integrated.

The major attribute is *Divine Creative Energies* which furnish the "fuel" for all actions and deeds in the Psyche and the World.

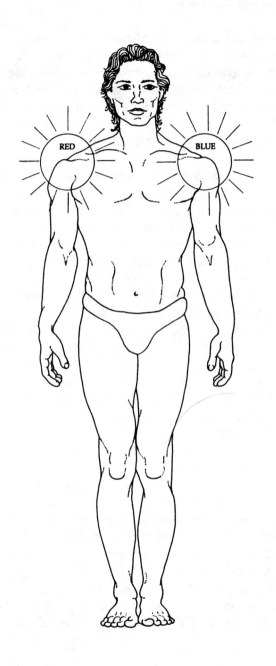

The final purpose of the Ritual of the Cross is to formulate and awaken a Great Cross of Light in the Candidate's Aura, by activating and lighting up the above mentioned Psychospiritual Centers with specific Divine Names that are vibrated and entoned therein, so that he can *visualize, sense, feel* and *experience* Light, Fire, and Life springing forth into consciousness, flowing through this Cross, and filling his being.

For a realization of this spiritual exercise, it is very important that the psychological and spiritual aspects be coordinated and integrated. That is, the subjective visualization (invocation) and the objective, awakening and manifestation (evocation) of the Light, Fire, and Life (the triune manifestations of the Spiritual Energies) be achieved by the Candidate.

To achieve these goals, the Candidate must not only see or visualize but also sense, feel, and experience the Light, Fire, and Life flowing through his Aura and Being, thereby consecrating himself as the Active and operational Channel for the Divine Spark to manifest Its Attributes at the conscious level. This implies that the Candidate has properly understood and mastered the principles and methodology that I have outlined in this work and has thus become a "Living Temple" for the Divine Spark which can now arise from Its "Inner Sanctuary" and manifest forth in the personality of the Candidate.

When the Divine Spark begins to arise, the Colors, the Vibrations, and the Energies of the activated Psychospiritual Center can awaken, manifesting forth into consciousness and blending with each other, activating the whole Tree of Life through a creative synthesis of which the whole is much greater than the sum of its parts.

This manifestation can only be fully realized when Concentration, Meditation, Contemplation, and Theurgy have been worked through by the use of the 7 functions of the Psyche and the Candidate has actually visualized, sensed, felt, and experienced, and thus *become,* the living cross of light-fire-creative energies which the Candidate is invoking and awakening.

What I am attempting to describe in very limited human words, is a much larger, greater and righter process which must be *lived* and *experienced* to be fully realized and understood, and which will itself reveal and unveil its mysteries and powers to the Candidate. Then, and only then, will the God within truly manifest and do the work and become the officiating priest and not the human ego of the Candidate!

It is at this point that the Sign of the Cross will become hot, alive, and truly operational in the Consciousness and Aura of the Candidate transforming his (or her) consciousness and enabling the Christ within to do His Work of personal and collective regeneration and redemption. It is also at this point that the Candidate will be able to use the Sign of the Cross to perform the five-fold functions we described in *The Nature and Use of Ritual for Spiritual Attainment,* namely:

1. As a means to consciously bring more Spiritual Light and Life to the Candidate, in order to link his human self with his Spiritual self.

2. As a means to achieve self-mastery and true Peace.

3. As a model par excellence for all creative processes and the means by which the Candidate's Self can express Itself consciously in the world.

4. As a means to awaken and activate all the Psychospiritual Centers on the Tree of Life, and thereby to eventually achieve true union with God or Illumination.

5. As a means to integrate Reality within one's being: God with Humanity and Nature and the inner with the outer worlds.

Once the Candidate has mastered the Ritual of the

Cross for himself and succeeded in making the Great Cross of Light become alive in his consciousness and reveal some of its more advanced mysteries to him, then he is ready to effectively use some of the variants of the Cross Ritual in his Circle of Light with other persons, or to pass from the *Invoking Cross* to the *Projecting Cross*.

Having formulated and awakened the Great Cross of Light in himself and visualized, sensed, felt and experienced its circulating Light, Fire, and Life, and the transformation of the consciousness brought about by the fusing and mingling of its colors, vibrations and energies, and once the Divine Spark in him has been awakened into consciousness and is now in charge of the further work, he can then proceed as shown on page 116.

The projected, greater Cross of Light should still be connected with the Cross of Light in his own Aura and with its Light, Fire, and Life-feeding Centers of the Head, Heart, and Shoulders so that Consciousness, Love and Life can constantly pour into it, as its combined energies flow back to him and enrich his inner Cross of Light.

Finally, the Candidate, another member of the Circle, or someone outside the Circle can be "projected" and "visualized" in the center of the Cross for healing or inspirational purposes, or additional rituals can be carried out with this "externalized Altar" as their focus.

Many more variants and uses of the Cross ritual do exist, but they will have to be discovered by the Candidate himself as he masters and uses the Invoking and Projecting Cross I have discussed earlier in this chapter, and as the Divine Spark in him will unfold and reveal the further treasures and mysteries of the "Life-giving Cross."

Visualize and project the cross of Light that blazes in your own Aura in the center of the Circle of Light, with the vertical arm expanding and thrusting towards the sky and center of the Earth; while the horizontal arm can spread forth and expand toward the four cardinal points is or blend in with the horizontal circle of light and expand to include the room and the community where the ritual is taking place.

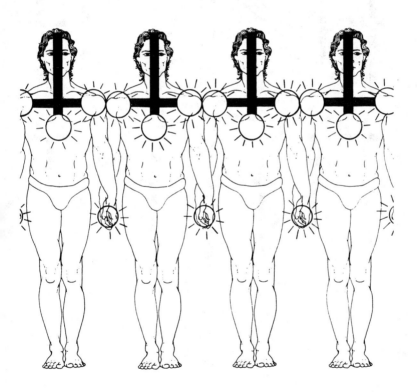

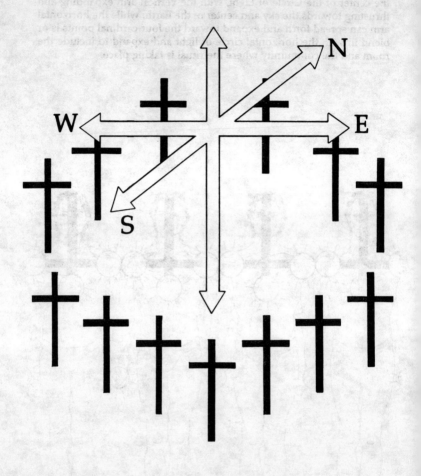

There should be at least seven participants in the Circle of Light, but no more than thirteen.

8
THE LORD'S PRAYER

Its Nature and Use

Text:
> Our Father who art in Heaven.
> Hallowed be Thy Name.
> Thy Kingdom Come.
> Thy will be done, on Earth as it is in Heaven.
> Give us this day our daily bread, and forgive us our trespasses as we forgive those who trespass against us.
> And lead us not into temptation but deliver us from evil (the Evil One).
> For Thine is the Kingdom, and the Power, and the Glory, of the Father, and of the Son, and of the Holy Spirit.
>
> Amen.

Up to this point the candidate has been learning, mastering and awakening the "tools of the trade," or to be more specific, developing the necessary cognitive framework, the essential philosophy, values and beliefs of the Great Work; and also gaining a greater understanding of the structure, functions, and essential 'muscles' of the Psyche and their proper utilization for the grand aim of Personal

Transformation and Spiritual Awakening which culminated in the mastery and awakening of the Great Cross of Light.

This could be compared to the laying down of the foundation of a house so that now the "house proper" can be built. This house is, in this context, the Human Temple, which is to be inhabited by the Divine Spark, Who then can consciously use it to do His work of completing it and working in the world to accomplish His own intentions.

With the Lord's Prayer the preparatory phase of the Work, the "Opening Ritual" comes to an end, and the true work, the "Closing Ritual," can begin and unfold.

The Lord's Prayer and the other Fundamentals of the Christian Tradition can all be used in a triune fashion or with the three basic foci of transformation and development:

1. In the microcosm, for the Candidate himself, for his Aura and Psychospiritual Centers;
2. For the Temple or persons making up the Circle of Light Generator, which acts as the bridge or connecting link, between the microcosm and the macrocosm.
3. For the world, the macrocosm.

Now the basic tools of the Great Work, the essential "muscles of human consciousness," and the use of Divine Names and the awakening of the Cross of Light can all (and must be) used synchronously in the work on the Lord's Prayer, and its utilization for Concentration, Meditation, Contemplation, and Theurgic work.

Before beginning the actual work on the Lord's Prayer, let the Candidate review the basic nature and functions of this universal spiritual exercise, reawakening them in his consciousness, and then focus his attention, thoughts, and feelings upon them. Essentially there are seven basic Petitions, or Formulae, each of which contain several basic Symbols,

Archetypes, or Names of Power that awaken and circulate the Light, Fire, and Life of the Divine spark, expressing through seven Signs of the Cross, each of which has its own precise and specific intention and objective.

It is most important to realize that it is the Divine Spark, the Spirit of God in us which, once awakened and brought forth into consciousness, will do this work, and act as the "Officiating Priest," and not our normal conscious human ego or personality!

Seen in this perspective, the Lord's Prayer is the cornerstone, the universal foundation, of all true spiritual work, expressed in the symbols and words of the Christian Tradition, to bring us in touch with the *Lord God* within each of us . . . and to attune our consciousness and will with those of the Divine Spark so that we may commune with Him at increasingly more conscious and intense levels, and thereby enable this Divine Spark to do His Work in us and in the world.

Herein lies a whole spiritual curriculum and training program by which to establish:

1. A right relationship with God, and to attain the Mysteries of the Holy Grail and the *Philosopher's Stone*, which is the key to the true knowledge of God, Man and Nature, and the Living Source of all Knowledge;
2. To attain the *Elixir Vitae*, the key to conscious Immortality and the very Source of Eternal life;
3. And to attain the *Panacea*, the universal medicine which can cure all ills, and its Living Source.

As such, the Lord's Prayer is an interrelated and organically designed set of symbols and formulae which contain both knowledge about man's psychospiritual anatomy and physiology, and an integrated set of practical exercises designed to awaken man's Psychospiritual Centers, train key faculties of the Psyche, and achieve Spiritual Illumination, Initiation, or Union with the Christ within. It must be activated in the Candidate's Field of Consciousness and from there bring to life and consciousness both the Unconscious and the Superconscious, personal and collective, through its language of Names of Power, Images, and Archetypes which act as consciousness and energy transformers.

Bear in mind that the central process that makes the Lord's Prayer as well as any other Prayer or Ritual "come alive" for oneself and others is Faith, the synthesis of Willing, Thinking, Feeling and Visualization.

The Lord's Prayer performs several important functions on different levels of Being and Reality.

> *Psychologically:* It can be used to understand and awaken one's Psyche, and to train its various functions.
>
> *Socially:* It can be used to unite and direct the aspirations, thoughts, feelings, and energies of a group of people (the members of the Circle of Light Generator and later others) and thus achieve an interpersonal Psychosynthesis, and social integration.
>
> *Spiritually:* It can perform seven different fundamental functions, eventually all leading and merging into one supreme function which enables the candidate to achieve Spiritual Illumination, Initiation, or Union with God, which is the ultimate goal of human evolution and the highest aim of all true Spiritual Training.

These seven different functions on the Spiritual Level are:

1. To provide the Candidate with a *living Source* of Knowledge.
2. To enable the Candidate to train and exercise various psychospiritual functions (thinking, willing,

imagination, feelings, biopsychic drives, sensations, and the intuition).

3. To progressively awaken, activate, and integrate all the psychospiritual Centers on the Tree of Life.

4. To establish a genuine breakthrough of the Super-conscious into the conscious, thus opening up a channel between the human and the Spiritual Self through which Light, Fire, and Life, Intuitions, Feelings and Energies can flow.

5. To feed and harmonize all the Candidate's "bodies" and their key faculties: spiritual, mental, emotional, and vital.

6. Progressively enable the Candidate to link his will with the Will of the Divine Spark within him so that the Latter may manifest Itself in the Psyche and in the world, to express therein the Attributes of the Higher Self: Divine Wisdom, Divine Love, and Divine Life.

7. To provide a safe and effective way of coming into contact with the Inner Worlds, the Celestial Hierarchies, and the Brotherhood of the Rosy Cross.

Practical work on the Lord's Prayer:

After the Candidate has gone through the preliminary phase of the work and the Opening Ritual, he can then, either by working alone or in a group (or both), begin to do the following in order to make the Lord's Prayer come alive for him:

1. Concentrate and Meditate upon each of the key symbols of the Lord's Prayer and then Contemplate and experience its "awakening" and response in your consciousness and being.

2. Concentrate and Meditate upon each petition of the Lord's Prayer and then contemplate and experience its impact on each of your Psychospiritual

Centers, Bodies, and level of consciousness.
3. Concentrate and Meditate upon the whole prayer and then contemplate and experience its impact upon your whole being, consciousness and daily life.
4. Use each petition of the Lord's Prayer for its Theurgic Impact upon your Tree of Life, Aura, and consciousness as a whole, and then for its impact upon the members of the Circle of Light, individually and collectively.
5. Finally, the candidate can make a time-study of the basic patterns of his life and consciousness, while using the Lord's Prayer in any of the previously suggested ways, observing how it brings about changes in his consciousness and behavior, no matter how subtle, and thus upon his being and that of others through his relationships with them.

The Candidate should then carefully and regularly write in his workbook and then in his diary what work he has done, and with what results, and what are the subtle and long-range transformations that have been taking place in his consciousness and life.

Following are the basic principles and key insights for working on each of the petitions for the Lord's Prayer in order that the Candidate may unveil its key meanings, correspondences, and applications in the microcosm and have a Theurgic Impact therein:

1. Our Father Who art in Heaven:

Our: We all come from the same Spiritual Source, and are made of the same Spiritual Essence; eventually, all of us shall achieve Union with the Spiritual

Self. Thus we are all Spiritual Brothers and Sisters, whose being, destiny, and well-being are all inter-linked.

Father: This Name represents the creative and life-sustaining Principle, the Spiritual Principle from whence we came, which sustains us while on Earth, and to which we shall return in full con-sciousness.

The Father is also the real, immortal, Spiritual, but as yet unknown Self. He is the Divine Spark, the Christ within, the Osiris, the Atman, the Lord, or whatever the God in Man is called.

Heaven: This is a higher, qualitatively different, state of consciousness than the one we normally func-tion in. It is the Superconscious or Spiritual Con-sciousness.

As a whole, this petition focuses our consciousness (aspirations, thoughts, feelings, visualizations, and energies) upon the Divine Spark, opening up a channel through which the Spiritual Energies (Light, Fire, and Life) can flow into our whole Aura and Tree of Life, establishing a break-through of the Superconscious into the conscious. In so doing, we "Light the Lamp on High" or "put on our Crown," that is, we activate *Kether*.

This petition leads us to the realization of God's Pres-ence and Power within our being and in the world. It blazes open a Path through which we can raise our consciousness to Him and thus enable Him, His Wisdom, Love, and Life to express in our being, in our lives and in the world.

We recommend that you use this petition regularly, both alone and in the Circle of Light Generator, for a certain period of time, say a month, and see what happens.

Record in your workbook what you did, when you did it, and what results were obtained. Then describe in your diary what happened to you during this period of time and how you reacted to and coped with your daily events, watching for subtle changes and transformations in your consciousness, your behavior, and in your ability to *live*.

Our Father Who art in Heaven

What meanings, correspondences, and applications did you get for each key symbol, and what images or experiences unfolded in your consciousness while you were doing so, or perhaps later?

What did you get for the Petition as a whole and what was its Theurgic impact upon your consciousness, Aura, and Tree of Life? Transcribe all this material into your workbook carefully and then proceed to the next petition.

Our:

Father:

Heaven:

Exercise: Focus all your thoughts on your Head Center, concentrate on the petition and vibrate it in your Head Center; then focus all your emotions and devotion upon your Heart Center, and slowly visualize these emotions rising up to your Head Center. Finally, focus your physical and etheric energies, and your Will, upon your Shoulder Centers and visualize these energies also rising up to your Head Center. At this time your whole Field of Consciousness should be focused upon your Head Center.

2. Hallowed be Thy Name

Hallowed be: this implies to be aware of, to enter into a proper relationship with, to give and to receive what is appropriate (Male and Female Polarities) and to *make whole or become holy.*

Thy Name: the Presence, Consciousness and Energies of the Divine Spark; for a Name is a representation of and a *path to* the Reality it denotes which, in this case, is the Divine Spark.

This petition reaffirms and extends the breakthrough of the Superconscious into the conscious that was affected by the first petition (Our Father Who Art in Heaven) and it calls forth or draws down the Light, Fire and Life of the Divine Spark to fill our whole Aura by one's hunger for and devotion to Him (the Divine Spark). Whereas with the first Petition we climbed onto the Holy Mountain of Consciousness to the place where the Divine Light and Presence dwell, with the present petition we draw down and bring back that Light and that Presence to the Field of Consciousness to suffuse and impregnate our whole being with Them (that is, our Spiritual, Mental, Emotional and Vital Bodies and their organs and functions).

With this Petition we now formulate the First Great Cross of Light, Fire and Life in our Aura and Tree of Life, distributing the Light and Energies of the Divine Spark, and thus *its Consciousness,* in all dimensions and aspects of our being.

This will help every "body," Center and subpersonality in our being, our little kingdom, to become aware of and enter into a right relationship with the down-pouring Energies

OUR FATHER WHO ART IN HEAVEN

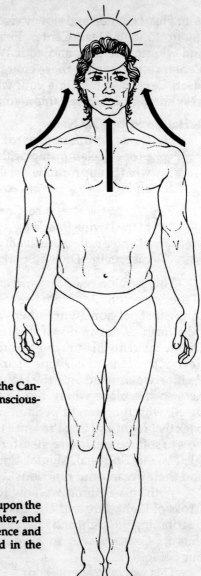

As this petition is vibrated by the Candidate or Priest, focus your consciousness, that is your:

Thoughts
Feelings
Energies
Aspirations
Imagination

in other words, all your Faith, upon the Divine Spark in the Head Center, and become aware of God's Presence and Power within your Being and in the world.

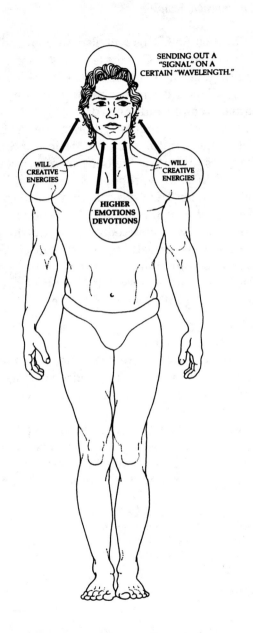

of the Spiritual Self. This will also awaken and "light-up" the *Chokmah* and *Binah* Centers (see illustration on page 129) slowly bringing His Consciousness and Presence in our being and life, purifying, sanctifying and perfecting both the Human Temple and the World.

Use this petition regularly, both alone and in the Circle of Light Generator, for a chosen period of time, and see what happens to you and the other members of the Circle.

Record in your workbook what you did, when and with what results. Then describe in your diary what happened to you during this period of time and how you reacted to and coped with your daily events, watching for subtle changes and transformations in your consciousness, your behavior, and your ability to *live*.

Use the Consciousness Checklist (see Appendix) as an inner, psychological measuring device.

Hallowed be Thy Name

What meanings, correspondences, and applications did you get for each key symbol, and what images or experiences unfolded in your consciousness while you were doing so and later?

What did you get for this petition as a whole and what was its Theurgic impact upon your consciousness, Aura, and Tree of Life? Transcribe all this information carefully into your workbook and then proceed to the next Petition.

Hallowed be:

Thy Name:

With this Petition we formulate the First Great Cross of Light, Fire and Life in our Aura and Tree of Life, distributing the Light and Energies of the Divine Spark through our entire being.

As we do this, we also "light up" *Chokmah* and *Binah,* thus slowly bringing His Consciousness and Presence in our being and in our life.

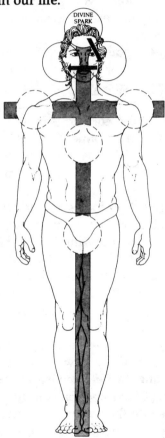

**Purifying and Sanctifying
The Aura and Energies
of The "Temple"**

Thy Kingdom Come

Thy: refers to the Divine Spark, the Spiritual Self or the Christ within.

Kingdom: this symbol literally means a King ruling over a body of human beings occupying a certain territory which is governed by certain laws.

Here the kingdom is your personality with its bodies, faculties, energies, resources, and many entities (sub-personalities).

Thus far, for you and in your life, the King (the Divine Spark) is not yet the Ruler or rules only in an indirect and partial way. The reason for this is that the channel, or connecting bridge, between the Super-conscious and the conscious is not fully developed and operative, the connection between the human and the Spiritual Self is tenuous and distorted, and your personality itself is not yet completed and well coordinated.

Thus, many other forces and principles are still ruling your being and life. Temporarily, you can change that and enthrone the King in your Little Kingdom.

Come: let the Light, Fire, and Life of the Divine Spark come into your being, be realized in your consciousness and life. That is, make the Spiritual Self become the King, the Lord, or synthesizing principle of *your* personality and life.

This petition as a whole again draws down the Divine Light, Fire and Life of the Divine Spark in a Cross-like fashion, formulating the Second Great Cross of Light, Fire and Life activating *Chesed* and transforming the Presence of the Divine Spark into the Rulership of the Divine Spark in all the levels of your consciousness, Aura, and Tree of Life so that He may manifest in your being and life.

This petition also helps us to realize and experience that the Kingdom of God is a *State of Consciousness* which must be attained within oneself and which will then radiate into, affect, and transform our personal, professional, social and spiritual life.

This Petition will also make us aware that this is the greatest goal and treasure a human being can, and must achieve here on Earth, in full consciousness, and it will also bring with this awareness the desire and strength to achieve it little by little.

Use this petition regularly, both alone and in the Circle of Light Generator, for a certain period of time, and see what happens to you and to the others. Record in your workbook what you did, when you did it, and with what results. Then describe in your diary what happened to you during this period of time and how you reacted to and coped wth your daily events, watching for subtle changes and transformations that might occur in your consciousness, your behavior, and in your ability to *live*.

Again, use the Consciousness Checklist as an inner, psychological measuring device.

Thy Kingdom Come

What meanings, correspondences, and applications did you get for each key symbol, and what images or experiences unfolded in your consciousness while you were doing so and later?

What did you get from the Petition as a whole, and what was its Theurgic impact upon your consciousness, Aura and Tree of Life?

Transcribe all of this information carefully and then proceed to the next Petition.

Thy:

Kingdom:

Come:

Thy Will Be done on Earth as It is in Heaven

> *Thy Will:* The Will or Focused Energies of the Divine Spark.
>
> *Be Done:* be accomplished, translated from the potentiality into actuality; brought from the level of an idea to that of a Lived Experience or brought into consciousness.
>
> *Earth:* your Field of Consciousness, conscious mind, and personality.
>
> *Heaven:* the Superconscious, the higher superliminal levels of consciousness, or Spiritual Consciousness, wherein one truly *knows* oneself, God, one's right relationships to others, and one's purpose here on Earth.

This Petition, through another "downpouring" of Spiritual Energies, continues and completes the process begun by the last Petition—Thy Kingdom Come.

If God's Kingdom is to be realized in our being, in our lives and finally in the world, His will must be known and accomplished as a prerequisite to achieve this Kingdom of God. God's Will (the Will of the Divine Spark) is always being accomplished in the Superconscious or in the spiritual nature of man, but not in his personality or conscious mind.

What takes place at the spiritual or Superconscious

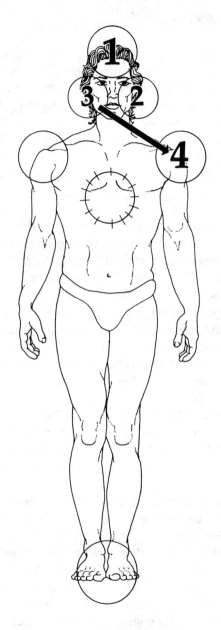

THY KINGDOM COME

levels must now be extended and projected downwards so that it might be realized at the personality level, or conscious level as well. For this to happen, the personality must long for this and cooperate in bringing this about. Once God's Presence has become conscious in us, His Creative Energies and Will can gradually become operative in our personality and life.

The basic thought-form contained in this Petition is designed to have us focus on this operation in order to enflesh it consciously.

This petition brings about another downpouring of Spiritual Energies which formulates the Third Great Cross of Light, Fire and Life and activates *Geburah*.

With this Third Great Cross the Intuition is activated, and the flow of Spiritual Consciousness and Energies now fuse with our aspirations, thoughts and feelings, spiritualizing them and thus transforming our words and actions.

The Word of Power—*Be Done*—here specifically refers to the transmission and transformation of the Divine Light through the various "bodies" to accomplish the purpose of the Spiritual Self.

Finally, this Petition also acts as the Theurgic formula to bring Energies of the Divine Spark to the Human Prism of the Head, Heart, and Shoulders or in another sense, from Heaven to Earth, from Spirit to Matter and from *Kether* to *Malkuth*.

Use this Petition regularly, both alone and in the Circle of Light, for a chosen period of time and see what happens to you and others.

Record in your workbook what you did, when you did it, and with what results. Then describe in your diary what happened to you during this period of time and how you reacted to and coped with your daily events, watching for subtle changes and transformations in your consciousness, your behavior, and in your ability to *live*.

Again use the Consciousness Checklist as an inner, psychological measuring device and ask your friends and Significant Others if they noticed any changes in you.

Thy Will Be Done on Earth as it is in Heaven

What meanings, correspondences, and applications did you get for each symbol, and what images or experiences unfolded in your consciousness while you were doing so and later?

What did you get from the Petition as a whole, and what was its Theurgic impact upon your consciousness, Aura, and Tree of Life?

Transcribe all of this information carefully and then proceed to the next Petition.

Thy Will:

Be Done:

Earth:

Heaven:

THY WILL BE DONE ON EARTH AS IT IS IN HEAVEN

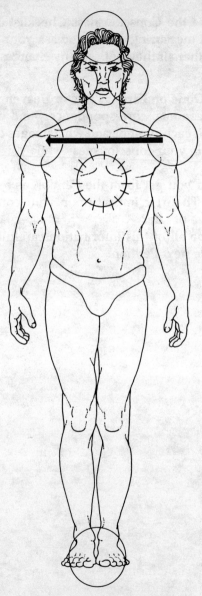

THY WILL BE DONE

Give Us This Day Our Daily Bread

> *Give Us:* suffuse our being (Aura and Tree of Life) and let us become aware of ...
>
> *This Day:* Now, wherever we happen to be: the present cycle in our life and evolution.
>
> *Daily Bread:* on the horizontal axis, the "Daily Bread" of our Soul is *Experience,* while on the vertical axis it is the *Divine Light.*

Every single day, in every cycle, and at every moment of our existence, the Divine Spark gives us the "Daily Bread" of our Soul which is *human experience.*

Unfortunately, we are not always conscious or aware of this "gift" from the Divine Spark so we do not understand what is happening to us or why we are living through our present situation, and therefore we cannot appreciate it and assimilate it fully.

Thus, on the vertical axis, this Petition Theurgically brings down the Divine Light into the Tree of Life and our Field of Consciousness to allow us to understand our daily experiences, to be able to assimilate these experiences more fully into our being, and thus to learn the lessons that these experiences bring to us.

This Petition also enables us to be grateful to God for our daily experiences, to receive them and accept them, no matter how unpleasant they may be, and to realize them as a gift of God and an opportunity for our human and spiritual growth.

The Theurgic aspect of this Petition manifests itself through a Fourth Great Cross of Light, Fire and Life flowing through our being and lighting up *Tiphareth* which shall make us more harmonious, centered, alive and aware of the great Gift that Life and its countless daily experiences truly are, and of the myriad opportunities that come our way to

GIVE US THIS DAY OUR DAILY BREAD

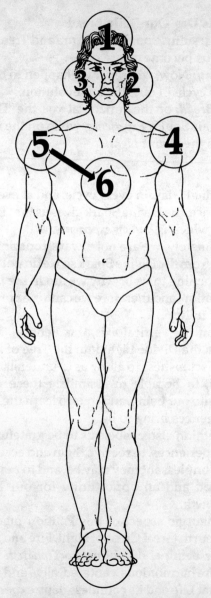

ON EARTH AS IT IS IN HEAVEN

learn to grow, to serve others and thus to live more consciously, creatively, and joyfully.

The Thought-form contained in this Petition opens up our consciousness and receptivity to the Divine Light, Fire, and Life pouring out from on high and to the World around us, thus helping us to become more alive, responsive and coordinated as a Living example of Life and Consciousness.

Use this petition regularly, both alone and in the Circle of Light for a certain period of time, and see what happens to you and the others.

Record in your workbook what you did, when, and with what results. Then, describe in your diary what happened to you during this period of time and how you reacted to and coped with your daily events, watching for subtle changes and transformations that might occur in your consciousness, your behavior, and your present ability to *live*.

Again you may use the Consciousness Checklist as an inner, psychological measuring device, and ask your friends and Significant Others if they noticed changes in you.

Give Us This Day our Daily Bread

What meanings, correspondences and applications did you get for each key symbol, and what images or experiences unfolded in your consciousness while you were doing so and later?

Give Us:

This Day:

Daily Bread:

What did you get from the Petition as a whole, and what was its Theurgic impact upon your consciousness, Aura, and Tree of Life?

Transcribe all of this information carefully and then proceed to the next Petition.

Forgive Us Our Trespasses As We Forgive Those Who Trespass Against Us

Forgive Us: the Spiritual Self *always* forgives us our trespasses and transforms our errors and mistakes into "learning experiences" and lessons that ultimately will benefit us and enable us to mature, to grow, and to transform our imperfections. Unfortunately, most of the time we are unaware of this and so must acquire this awareness.

Trespasses: these imply the violation of physical, psychological, social, and spiritual laws, whether they be in deeds, words, emotions, thoughts, or aspirations.

This Petition makes us aware of a most important universal Law: that of action and reaction, cause and effect, or Karma, which takes place on three basic levels:

1. Between the Superconscious and the Conscious Mind, or the Spiritual and Human Self.
2. Between our state of consciousness and our deeds, between our thoughts and our actions.
3. Between ourselves and the world, which includes other human beings, animals and nature; between the subjective and the objective dimensions of life.

This Petition unveils for us *experientially* that what we do unto others, ultimately we do unto ourselves, and that any objective action in the world is followed by a subjective reaction in our soul and consciousness.

Theurgically, this Petition demonstrates experientially that, as we forgive others we also forgive ourselves, and thus become aware that the Divine Spark, too, has forgiven us.

In this world we constantly violate a number of physical, psychological, social, and spiritual laws, some of which we are aware of and others that we are yet unaware of.

True forgiveness implies a great deal more than simply affirming: "I forgive you, let us begin anew in a different frame of mind." It implies mental understanding, emotional release, behavioral acceptance, and a psychospiritual transformation and unfolding a new perspective. It also involves "unclogging" psychospiritual Centers, transmuting many thoughts, emotions, and energies, and experientially changing our state of mind. When this truly occurs, unbalanced forces, negative thoughts, emotions, and energies in our Aura and Tree of Life are dissolved ... which facilitates genuine communication with others who come to us with their own problems and resentments.

Theurgically, this Petition implies transforming Vices into Virtues and thus performing a genuine alchemical operation in ourselves and in others.

This alchemical operation is made possible by another downpouring of Spiritual Energies which spread and diffuse themselves through the Fifth Great Cross of Light, Fire and Life in our Aura and Tree of Life. Its focus this time is the activation and "lighting up" of *Netzach*. In its wake this further outpouring of Spiritual Energies brings a playfulness, a lightness, a tolerance, and a flexibility which are not weakness or unconcern about what is happening, but a proper perspective and response ... which are unmistakable by the joyfulness and exhuberance they make possible in the person who has truly forgiven himself and others.

FORGIVE US OUR TRESPASSES, AS WE FORGIVE THOSE WHO TRESPASS AGAINST US.

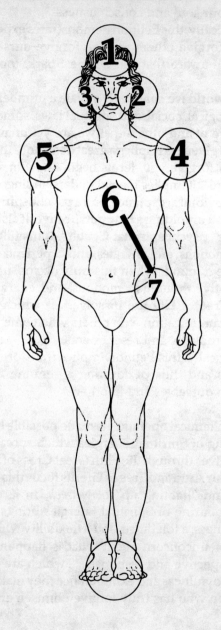

Use this Petition regularly, both alone and in the Circle of Light, for a chosen period of time, and see what happens to you and to the others in the Circle.

Record in your workbook what you did, when, and with what results. Then describe in your diary what happened to you during this period of time and how you reacted to and coped with your daily events, watching for subtle changes and transformations in your consciousness, your behavior, and in your present ability to *live*.

Again you may use the Consciousness Checklist as an inner, psychological measuring device, and ask your friends and Significant Others if they noticed changes in you.

Forgive Us Our Trespasses As We Forgive Those Who Trespass Against Us
What meanings, correspondences, and applications did you get for each key symbol, and what images or experiences unfolded in your consciousness while you were doing so and later?

Forgive:

Trespasses:

Lead Us Not Into Temptation But Deliver Us From Evil:

Lead Us Not: Make us aware of, recognize, and be

grateful for . . . *temptations*!

Deliver Us: Give us the awareness, understanding, and strength to overcome Temptations, Tests, or Ordeals, and to learn the lessons they contain.

Temptations: The great Tests, Ordeals, and Difficulties of Life which we need to face and to overcome to know ourself, our strengths, weaknesses and potential. Our Life here on Earth is composed of countless and varied situations, experiences, and tests designed to actualize our potential and to reveal to us our own nature, energies, and capacities, and later the Power of God to heal us, resurrect us, and transform Evil into Good.

Evil (One): This is none other than our Lower Self: unbalanced forces, negative thoughts desires, emotions and energies in our being which must be "conquered," and eventually transformed into a pure set of vehicles and energies for the Higher Self which will then put them to work for His own purposes.

Of all the Petitions of the Lord's Prayer, this is the one that is apt to be misunderstood, probably because of a poor translation from the original words and meanings.

The spiritual Self never leads us into temptation, rather it is the lower self which does this. Temptations and tests abound in life and are *necessary* for our human and spiritual development! The key is to be aware that a temptation or test is an ordeal sent *for our benefit*, and to have the consciousness and strength to resist it and pass it successfully. Temptations and tests are myriad and of many different types. Some are physical while others are emotional, mental, and even spiritual in nature; some are within our power to resist while others are not and can be overcome only with Spiritual Assistance.

This Petition, therefore, is an invocation to the spiritual Energies (Light, Life, and Fire) to help us recognize temp-

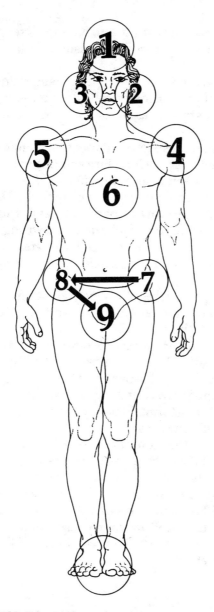

LEAD US NOT INTO TEMPTATION BUT DELIVER US FROM EVIL.

tations for what they truly are, to have the strength to withstand their onslaught, and the wisdom to be grateful for them.

Basically, there are two types of temptations or tests: those created by our lower self (the great majority) and those sent to us by God as an "ordeal" and our next "lesson" on the Path.

The Theurgic aspect of this petition manifests through a Sixth Great Cross of Light, Fire and Life in our Aura and Tree of Life, activating and "lighting up" *Hod* and *Yesod* respectively, and enabling us to overcome the Dark Side of our nature, the Shadow or personal Devil, which is composed of the accretion of all our vices, wrong deeds and negative thoughts, emotions, and energies accumulated and crystallized in our unconscious over a long period of time.

Use this petition regularly, both alone and in the Circle of Light for a certain period of time, and see what happens to you and to others.

Record in your workbook what you did, when, and with what results. Then describe in your diary what happened to you during this period of time and how you reacted to and coped with your daily events, watching for subtle changes and transformations in your consciousness, your behavior, and your present ability to *live*.

Again, use the Consciousness Checklist as an inner, psychological measuring device and ask your friends and Significant Others if they noticed any changes in you.

What meanings, correspondences, and applications did you get for each key symbol, and what images and experiences unfolded in your consciousness, Aura, and Tree of Life? Transcribe all this carefully and then proceed to the next Petition.

Deliver Us:

Temptation:

Evil (One):

For Thine is the Kingdom, and the Power, and the Glory, of the Father, the Son, and of the Holy Spirit; Always, Now and Forever and Unto the Ages of Ages. Amen.

> *For Thine:* The Kingdom, our Personality, ultimately is of and for the Divine Spark, the Christ within.
>
> *Kingdom:* Your conscious mind, personality, body, life and *Malkuth.*
>
> *Power:* This refers to certain spiritual Energies and Impulses activated in *Geburah* expressing the Will and Justice of God.
>
> *Glory:* This refers to other spiritual Energies and impulses activated in *Chesed* expressing the love and Mercy of God.
>
> *Father, Son, and Holy Spirit:*
> These are the Trinity, One in Essence and Threefold in manifestation, that is : Light expressing as Divine Wisdom, Fire expressing as Divine Love, and Life expressing as Divine Creative Energies.

This final Petition "fixes" the Great Cross of Light, Fire, and Life which has been awakened and formulated through successive outpourings and downpourings of spiritual Energies which have activated and lit up all the Psychospiritual Centers upon the Aura of the Candidate who now "wears it on his breast" . . . when he has become a true Initiate.

This Petition also reaffirms in symbols and builds up a final Thought-form asserting (and thus bringing about in the inner worlds) that the Kingdom and its Powers (Man's conscious mind, personality, life, and the Functions of his Psyche) are of and for the spiritual Self to become conscious of Itself and to manifest Its attributes of Divine Wisdom, Divine Love, and Divine Creative Energies in Man and in the World.

This Petition is both the culmination and the completion of the Lord's Prayer and the Christian version of the Qabalistic Cross.

As the Lord's Prayer began with the Cross Ritual, so it ends with it. At this point, you have "come down" the entire Tree of Life through the "Path of the Flaming Sword" and this Seventh Great Cross of Light, Fire, and Life brings down the combined spiritual Energies of all the psycho-spiritual Centers focusing them upon *Malkuth*, awakening it, activating it, and dedicating it to the Great Work of spiritual regeneration, the Work of the Divine Spark or of the Spirit of God which it must reflect and perform in this world.

The Initiates of Ancient Greece, in their Mystery Traditions, claimed that Divinity is entombed in Nature, that Divinity sleeps spellbound in Man, and that Man's greatest and highest labor here on Earth was to break the spell and open that tomb, so that the Divine could reawaken and manifest consciously Its Attributes in Creation.

The Lord's Prayer is one of the central practical keys to accomplish this Herculean Labor. But as the Lord's Prayer is made living and effective by Man's Faith, as it *reflects Man's level of evolution and consciousness in how it is used and interpreted*, Man will probably have to use it thousands of times before its true import and practical effects can be discerned and applied efficaciously.

You, the reader and Candidate to the Great Work, have an opportunity to work Consciously and Systematically at making the Lords' Prayer be "hot," "alive," and "effective" in your life progressively unveiling its many mysteries and treasures.

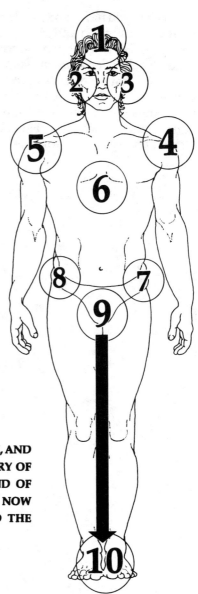

FOR THINE IS THE KINGDOM, AND
THE POWER, AND THE GLORY OF
THE FATHER, THE SON, AND OF
THE HOLY SPIRIT; ALWAYS, NOW
AND FOREVER, AND UNTO THE
AGES OF AGES. AMEN.

When you have successfully accomplished this endeavor, your own Intuition and inner channels of communication with your Self will be opened and you will no longer need external teachers or manuals such as the present one.

Until that time, it is suggested that at least once a year you go through the entire Lord's Prayer following the guidelines I have described and that you record carefullly your results . . . which will also be a measure of your own human and spiritual growth.

9
THE NICENE CREED

Its Nature and Use

The Nicene Creed

>Wisdom! Stand up! Hear ye the symbol of our Holy Faith.

>I believe in One God the Father Almighty, Maker of Heaven and Earth, and of all things visible and invisible.

>And in one Lord Jesus Christ, the only begotten Son of God; Begotten of His Father, before all ages, Light of Light; Very God of Very God; begotten not made; being of one essence with the Father: By Whom all things were made. Who for us men and for our salvation came down from Heaven and was incarnate by the Holy Ghost and of the Virgin Mary. And became Man.

>And was crucified also for us under Pontius Pilate; He suffered and was buried.

>And the third day He rose again according to the Scriptures.

>And ascended into Heaven and sitteth on the Right Hand of the Father.

And He shall come again, with Glory to judge both the quick and the dead; whose Kingdom shall have no end.

And in the Holy Ghost, the Lord, the Giver of Life: Who precedeth from the Father: Who with the Father and the son is worshipped and glorified: Who spake by the prophets.

And in One Holy Catholic and Apostolic Church.

I acknowledge one baptism for the remission of sins.

I look for the resurrection of the dead.

And the Life of the ages to come.

Amen.

The Nicene Creed embodies, in symbolic language, both the essence of the Christian Faith and the central Principles and Truths of the Holy Wisdom or Primordial Tradition.

As we unveil its progressive levels of meaning, the Nicene Creed unfolds for us a map of what we can find for ourselves, experientially, in the higher states of Spiritual Consciousness. Thus, the Creed indicates the most important Principles and Truths concerning Reality, (both in Man and in the World); concerning God, Man, and Nature, the Divine Spark, the Soul, the Church, and Human and Spiritual Evolution.

The Nicene Creed tells us Who and What we *are*, why we are living here on Earth, and what we are destined to become. Thus, it deals with the most important questions a human being can ask about himself, the universe, life, and Reality. Like the Emerald Tablet or the Tarot, The Nicene Creed is a genuine, synthetic compendium of what the Ancients rightfully called *Wisdom* with as many different levels of meaning, implications, and applications as there are different levels of consciousness and being.

A child, an average person, a philosopher, a Saint, a Mystic, and a Master can all learn and profit from it, but in different degrees and ways.

What we are concerned with in this work is *your* personalized set of meanings, implications, and applications that this document can have for you, at this point in your life. We must stress that this is something that only you can realize for yourself by planting these "symbols," or "seeds," and their formulae in your consciousness and being. To this end, the perspectives, insights, and methodology suggested in this Handbook can be most useful. Don't ever forget that *you* are the *essential* and *final* laboratory to test and refine whatever we are proposing to you.

At this point, we would expect you to have mastered fairly well the fundamentals we have suggested to you and that you can apply them for whatever task you choose.

Let's apply them to make the Nicene Creed come alive and reveal its Wisdom, Mysteries, and Treasures so that you may acquire, live and become its wisdom!

To do this, you must enter your personal or collective Temple, by yourself or in the Circle of Light and then:

1. Visualize your Aura,
2. Visualize and formulate your Tree of Life with its Psychospiritual Centers, lighting them up and activating them through one or more of the previous spiritual exercises.
3. Go through the Consciousness Checklist systematically to bring into consciousness and activate the seven Functions of the Psyche and their "muscles."
4. Finally, apply the four basic stages of the Work of Personal Transformation, Consciousness Expansion,

and Spiritual Awakening:
> Concentration
> Meditation
> Contemplation
> Theurgy

to each of the Symbols, or consciousness and energy transformers, and to all of the formulae of this great and timeless Document.

5. Then, write carefully what you did, when, and what results you obtained in your workbook and keep a careful account of your daily events and your interpretation and reactions to them in your diary.

In the Eastern Orthodox version of the Nicene Creed (which is the one we have adopted for this work), there are 12 basic formulae or essential Principles that are vibrated and which make up this Document as a whole.

1. I believe in One God the Father Almighty, Maker of Heaven and Earth, and of all Things Visible and Invisible.

This affirmation re-awakens inwardly the belief in, and for the Initiate, *the experience of* the Cosmic God, the Infinite Ocean of Light, Fire, and Life Who brought all Planes of Creation and of Man into being, the Spiritual Plane as well as the Physical Plane, the visible and the invisible.

By bringing into consciousness our belief in and experience of the Cosmic God, we automatically expand our consciousness, raise our vibrations, and enter in rapport with Him, thus we link our being and consciousness to the whole of Reality (and not just a part of It) and its ultimate Source and Essence.

Vibrate and intone this formula inwardly and/or outwardly and see what happens.

What meanings, correspondences, and applications do you get at this point?

What images or experiences does this Formula evoke for you?

What transformations of consciousness, energy, and behavior does this Formula bring about for you?

What visions, panoramas, or inner reality does this Formula unfold in your consciousness and being?

Make sure to record all this accurately as soon as possible after you have *lived it*, and then proceed to the next Formula.

2. **And in One Lord, Jesus Christ, the only begotten Son of God; Begotten of His Father, before all ages, Light of Light; very God of Very God: Begotten not made; being of one Essence and with the Father By Whom all things were made.**

Exoterically, in the world and in history, this statement claims that Jesus Christ is the One Lord, the Son of God Who is One with the Father.

Esoterically, in Man and in the microcosm, It shows the nature of the Divine Spark that is *your true self.* The Divine Spark should be (and will be) our Lord and Ruler, the integrating and unifying principle of our Psyche and actions.

It is the Divine Spark of every human being Who is the "Only Begotten Son of God" and not our vehicles of expression (the spiritual, mental, emotional, vital and physical body which are *created,* or fashioned, by the Divine Spark, as the snail makes its own shell, from the Substance and Energy of each Plane of Being).

The Divine Spark existed long before the world, Man's

bodies, matter and energy, time and space came into being. The Divine Spark is the Spirit of Man, the Light, Fire, and Life, and an integral part of the Infinite Ocean of Light, Fire, and Life that manifest the cosmic Spirit. Thus it is Divine in its origin and an integral part of the Spirit Which made all things.

Vibrate and intone this formula inwardly and/or outwardly and see what happens.

What meanings, correspondences, and applications do you get at this point?

What images or experiences does this Formula evoke for you?

What transformations of consciousness, energy, and behavior does this Formula bring about for you?

What visions, panoramas, or inner reality does this Formula unfold in your consciousness and being?

Make sure to record all this accurately as soon as possible after you have *lived it,* and then proceed to the next Formula.

3. **Who for us men and for our salvation came down from Heaven, and was incarnate of the Holy Ghost and of the Virgin Mary, and became Man.**

This affirmation continues what the previous one began.

Exoterically, it tells us about the historical Jesus the Christ and His Mission:

That Christ came down from the Spiritual Worlds to make possible our Salvation;

That He was fathered by the Holy Spirit and born of the Theotokus, and

That He became Man.

Esoterically, however, it tells us more about our Divine Spark:

That It came from the Spiritual Worlds and slowly involved into our vehicles, or "bodies," where It now lies asleep;

That It will be *born into our Souls,* into our human consciousness which will then experience the dawning of true Spiritual Consciousness by the Power of the Holy Spirit; and,

That It will finally live in us and manifest Its Attributes and Will through our bodies as It did in the God-Man Jesus Christ, Who is our prototype and archetype.

Vibrate and intone this formula inwardly and/or outwardly and see what happens.

What meanings, correspondences, and applications do you get at this point?

What images or experiences does this Formula evoke for you?

What transformations of consciousness, energy, and behavior does this Formula bring about for you?

What visions, panoramas, or inner reality does this Formula unfold in your consciousness and being?

Make sure to record all this accurately as soon as possible after you have *lived it,* and then proceed to the next Formula.

4. And was crucified also for us under Pontius Pilate; He suffered and was buried.

Jesus the Christ was crucified in the reign of Pontius Pilate, (a Roman Governor of what is now Israel, Jordan and Lebanon). Like other men, He suffered, but He knew *why* He was suffering, and He was buried.

The Divine Spark in us is also "crucified" on the Cross of Matter; the present level of development and coordination of our bodies and our present state of consciousness do not enable It to express Itself any more than our present social system and public consciousness enable a truly inspired human being to speak and to act in accordance with the dictates of his higher Consciousness and thus "crucify Him." The Divine Spark is thus buried entombed and imprisoned in all of us and It "suffers" as It cannot express Itself and manifest Its will and Attributes through our Human Temple.

Vibrate and intone this formula inwardly and/or outwardly and see what happens.

What meanings, correspondences, and applications do you get at this point?

What images or experiences does this Formula evoke for you?

What transformations of consciousness, energy, and behavior does this Formula bring about for you?

What visions, panoramas, or inner reality does this Formula unfold in your consciousness and being?

Make sure to record all this accurately as soon as possible after you have *lived it*, and then proceed to the next Formula.

5. And the third day he rose again according to the Scriptures.

Exoterically, the New Testament tells us that Jesus Christ resurrected after three days, came to life again and rent the tomb in the rock where His body was lain.

Esoterically, in our Tree of Life, the Divine Spark and true Spiritual Consciousness will also be "resurrected"; They will come to life again and permeate our whole human consciousness when the "third Day" will begin.

The first Day: was our animal or biological evolution phase,

The second Day: is our human and psychological evolution,

The third Day: is our spiritual evolution, on the threshold of which we now find ourselves.

Such is what the unwritten Holy Tradition or Hagia Sophia tells us.

Vibrate and intone this formula inwardly and/or outwardly and see what happens.

What meanings, correspondences, and applications do you get at this point?

What images or experiences does this Formula evoke for you?

What transformations of consciousness, energy, and behavior does this Formula bring about for you?

What visions, panoramas, or inner reality does this Formula unfold in your consciousness and being?

Make sure to record all this accurately as soon as possible after you have *lived it*, and then proceed to the next Formula.

6. And ascended into Heaven and sitteth on the right hand of the Father.

Exoterically, we are told by the New Testament that Jesus Christ ascended into Heaven and is now "sitting " on the right hand of the Father God.

Esoterically, this means that when the Divine Spark has indrawn into our Soul, or our invisible body, and when Spiritual Consciousness has dawned, It will link us up *consciously* with the Universal spirit (the Father) and with Cosmic Consciousness (the Kingdom of Heaven) which is our true home and state of consciousness. In other words, when a breakthrough of the Superconscious into the conscious occurs, then something (Spiritual Light, Fire, and Life) flows down into the center of our being and consciousness. And, when It reascends from whence It came, into the Superconscious, It will elevate our whole being with It and bring the very center of our consciousness and being back into the Superconscious or the Spiritual Realms.

Vibrate and intone this formula inwardly and/or outwardly and see what happens.

What meanings, correspondences, and applications do you get at this point?

What images or experiences does this Formula evoke for you?

What transformations of consciousness, energy, and behavior does this Formula bring about for you?

What visions, panoramas, or inner reality does this Formula unfold in your consciousness and being?

Make sure to record all this accurately as soon as possible after you have *lived it*, and then proceed to the next Formula.

7. **And He shall come again, with the Glory to judge both the Quick and the Dead; Whose Kingdom shall have no end.**

The Scriptures and the Church Tradition tell us that Jesus Christ will come again during the famous Judgement Day to judge all those who are alive and those who are "dead." From that point onwards the Millenium will be here and His Kingdom shall have no end.

However, in the microcosm this statement refers again to the Divine Spark in us and to Spiritual Consciousness.

Spiritual Consciousness first appears in a flash and then disappears to reappear when we least expect It. Eventually it will come back with spiritual Light that will surround our being (with "glory"). At which time, (through the perspective of a heightened consciousness) we shall look upon all of our actions, words and decisions, both past and present, in quite a different light than we do in a normal state of consciousness, and we shall evaluate them with a different set of criteria.

It is not an outside God or Power Who will judge us, and our lives, words and deeds, but our own Higher Self taking the true love of God and of our fellow human beings (and our spiritual growth and progress) as His yardstick.

Quick and the Dead: can be seen as meaning two basic things:
1. the things we did and remember, and the things we did but do not remember.
2. the things we did when we were illuminated by Spiritual Consciousness, and the things we did in our "normal" state of consciousness.

Whose Kingdom Shall Have No End: When the Divine Spark takes control of our being and lives, and when Spiritual consciousness illuminates our stream of awareness, two basic things happen:
1. We cease to live in the Past and in the Future, and we live fully in the Present (one steps outside the track and prison of Time to *enter the eternal now*).
2. We acquire conscious immortality or a continuity of consciousness which is no longer broken by the cycles of birth and death, sleep and waking, and the rapidly narrowing and vanishing band of memory.

Vibrate and intone this formula inwardly and/or outwardly and see what happens.

What meanings, correspondences, and applications do you get at this point?

What images or experiences does this Formula evoke for you?

What transformations of consciousness, energy, and behavior does this Formula bring about for you?

What visions, panoramas, or inner reality does this Formula unfold in your consciousness and being?

Make sure to record all this accurately as soon as possible after you have *lived it,* and then proceed to the next Formula.

8. **And in the Holy Ghost, the Lord, the giver of Life: Who proceedeth from the father; Who with the Father and the Son together is worshipped and glorified: Who spake by the Prophets.**

Exoterically, this passage affirms our belief in the Third Person of the Holy Trinity, the Holy Spirit, Who is the Spirit of Truth, the Giver and Ruler of Life, Who *proceeds* from the Father and is *bestowed* by the Son, and Who with Them should be worshipped and glorified. Finally, it asserts that it is the same Spirit of Truth Who inspired and spoke through the countless genuine Prophets and Seers of humanity.

Esoterically, by affirming the reality of the Holy Spirit and by directing our focused attention, thoughts, and feelings to Him, this affirmation tunes us in to the Presence and Power of the Holy Spirit. It makes us vibrate as it were, on His wave-length, and thus develops a psychic channel through which He can manifest and work through our consciousness.

The Holy Spirit is One Manifestation of the Universal Spirit or Divine Light, Which is One in Essence, but Three in expression.

This specific expression of the Universal Spirit is the "Giver of Life," the Power that quickens, energizes and vivifies all It comes in contact with:

When it flows to our Head Center, It brings Truth
(which is why He is also called the "Spirit of Truth");
When It flows through our Heart Center, It quickens
and intensifies our feelings and Love;
When It flows through our Shoulders, It vivifies and
amplifies our Creative Energies or vitality.

On the Tree of Life, the Centers through which It
manifests are
Binah, in the Macrocosm;
Chesed and *Geburah,* at the Superconscious Level;
Yesod, at the conscious level in the microcosm.

It is Divine Wisdom and Divine Love that beget Divine
Life and Divine Creative Energy, Which in turn beget Truth,
Goodness, and Justice which are Divine Beauty and Har-
mony focused in *Tiphareth.*

First, humanity received the religion of the Father
through Jehova, then the religion of the son through Jesus
Christ, and now it is the religion of the Holy Spirit that we
are personally and collectively called to bring about through
the realization of the Great Work! This is what Jesus promised us as His greatest Gift.

While the religion of the Father and the Son was essentially a "faith religion" (that is a *non-experiential* religion)
without the personal experience and realization of its basic
tenets and truths, the religion of the Holy Spirit, which is
now in the process of "seeing light" or "being born," will be
essentially an experiential religion, one in which each individual will have, and must have a *direct* and *firsthand*
experience and realization of the Principles and Truths represented symbolically by the former religion.

This is why the religion of the Holy Spirit must be
integrated with Science and be a "scientific religion." In
other words, the coming religion of the Holy Spirit will be a
Path of Spiritual Initiation, leading its practitioners and

devotees to genuine Spiritual Illumination—which has always been foreshadowed and promised by the former. For it is through the quickening, vivifying and Life-giving Power of the Holy Spirit that the Tree of Life is "lit up," that the key Psychospiritual Centers are activated, and that the higher states of consciousness are effectively *brought through*.

Like the Power and Center of the Father and the Son, so the Power of the Holy Spirit and Its Centers must be "filled with Light, Fire, and Life," activated and brought into proper function in the Aura, or Sphere of Sensation, of the individual. For then, and only then, as the Holy Spirit inspired and spoke through the Prophets, Initiates, and the Adepts of Old, so I will now generate a breakthrough of the Superconscious into the conscious and It will inspire and speak through the candidate!

Vibrate and intone this formula inwardly and/or outwardly and see what happens.

What meanings, correspondences, and applications do you get at this point?

What images or experiences does this Formula evoke for you?

What transformations of consciousness, energy, and behavior does this Formula bring about for you?

What visions, panoramas, or inner reality does this Formula unfold in your consciousness and being?

Make sure to record all this accurately as soon as possible after you have *lived it*, and then proceed to the next Formula.

9. And in One Holy Catholic and Apostolic Church.

Esoterically, this affirmation can be interpreted in quite a different version than in its exoteric version. There is indeed, One Church or Religion that is truly *Holy*, (that is whole and complete) that is truly *Catholic* (meaning universal) and of which Apostolic Christianity was an external and symbolic representation on Earth. But this Holy and Catholic Religion, this Path of Spiritual Initiation and Illumination, that has existed from the first appearance of Man on Earth and which will remain with us till the whole of Humanity will have completed its Earthly evolution, *has never been and never will be fully incarnated or institutionalized on Earth*. For it is the One Source and Trunk from which all organized religions have drawn their deepest insights, their loftiest thoughts, and their living source of inspiration as they always will. But they will never be able to monopolize It and express It more than partially and in some aspects of Its infinite, living, unfolding Source.

This religion is no more and no less than the Inner Church, the Church Triumphant, the Communion of Saints, the true brotherhood of the Rosy Cross, or the Assembly of the Adepts of the Spirit. Its deepest living Sanctuaries on Earth are the hearts and the human consciousness of the true Mystics and Initiates Who walk the Earth amidst ordinary human beings. Its symbols and external manifestations can be found in all the Sacred Traditions and the Great World Religions. This Religion is the true and living repository of the Primordial Tradition, the *Hagia Sophia!*

Its major image or injunction is that given by Jesus when He said to Peter: "And Thou art Peter, and on this Rock I shall build My Church," when Jesus had asked him "Who am I?"

Peter had answered: "Thou art the Christ, the Son of the Living God."

What transpired here is the following: it was the Divine Spark in Peter Which enabled him to recognize the activated Divine Spark or Divinity of Jesus. Jesus, in turn, then affirmed that His Living Church would be made up of all those human beings, men and women, in whom the

Divine Spark had been awakened and who, by a breakthrough of the Superconscious into the conscious, can recognize the Living God in others and in the world—of the true Initiates and spiritually awakened human beings.

Vibrate and intone this formula inwardly and/or outwardly and see what happens.

What meanings, correspondences, and applications do you get at this point?

What images or experiences does this Formula evoke for you?

What transformations of consciousness, energy, and behavior does this Formula bring about for you?

What visions, panoramas, or inner reality does this Formula unfold in your consciousness and being?

Make sure to record all this accurately as soon as possible after you have *lived it*, and then proceed to the next Formula.

10. I acknowledge one Baptism for the remission of Sins.

Exoterically, this affirmation has been interpreted to mean that only the Baptism of the Christian Faith, and sometimes of even only one Christian Church, is valid to wash away one's Sins!

Esoterically, there is but one baptism or opening of a key psychospiritual Center, *Malkuth*, purification of the Aura, and transformation of human consciousness (willing, thinking, feeling, desiring, speaking, and acting) through the opening of a channel by which Spiritual Energies can flow into the Psyche, and that is the downpouring of spiritual energies in response to a deep need of the human heart, mind, and will, when the candidate is ready for this.

Vibrate and intone this formula inwardly and/or outwardly and see what happens.

What meanings, correspondences, and applications do you get at this point?

What images or experiences does this Formula evoke for you?

What transformations of consciousness, energy, and behavior does this Formula bring about for you?

What visions, panoramas, or inner reality does this Formula unfold in your consciousness and being?

Make sure to record all this accurately as soon as possible after you have *lived it*, and then proceed to the next Formula.

11. I look for the Resurrection of the Dead.

Exoterically, this was interpreted to mean that those who had died would come back to life or be resurrected at the legendary Final Judgement.

Esoterically, it has several meanings, the most important of which are:

1. That the many faculties and spiritual powers of Man which are presently dormant will be awakened and brought back to life by the quickening power of the Holy Spirit;

2. That many of the things we have done, said, and experienced in the past but forgotten will be remembered and brought to light or consciousness when the Spiritual Consciousness will illuminate us;

3. That eventually Man will acquire Spiritual Consciousness, Life Eternal or conscious immortality and thus be resurrected from the dead.

This resurrection will take place at different times and

in different degrees along the Path of spiritual evolution. It does occur, to a certain extent, when we pass on to the other side and when we pray with great fervor, or when we consciously receive the Sacraments, the Eucharist in particular. However, Its fullest and highest form will take place at the time of your Spiritual Initiation.

Vibrate and intone this formula inwardly and/or outwardly and see what happens.

What meanings, correspondences, and applications do you get at this point?

What images or experiences does this Formula evoke for you?

What transformations of consciousness, energy, and behavior does this Formula bring about for you?

What visions, panoramas, or inner reality does this Formula unfold in your consciousness and being?

Make sure to record all this accurately as soon as possible after you have *lived it*, and then proceed to the next Formula.

12. And the Life of the Ages to come.

Exoterically, this implies that Man's consciousness does not perish at death and still lives on in another dimension.

Esoterically, it continues and completes the foregoing affirmation, pointing to the fact that all human beings will continue their spiritual evolution and eventually attain conscious immortality or Life Eternal.

Vibrate and intone this formula inwardly and/or outwardly and see what happens.

What meanings, correspondences, and applications do you get at this point?

What images or experiences does this Formula evoke for you?

What transformations of consciousness, energy, and behavior does this Formula bring about for you?

What visions, panoramas, or inner reality does this Formula unfold in your consciousness and being?

Make sure to record all this accurately as soon as possible after you have *lived it*, and then proceed to the next Formula.

Whenever you attend Mass or hear the Creed being recited in a Church, use it Theurgically in your consciousness. Watch carefully and then record accurately all the images, experiences, meanings, correspondences, and energy or consciousness transformations this will trigger in you, recreating this inner reality and the *lived experience* of these fundamental truths about Reality and yourself.

Once a month, do a full Meditation, Concentration, and Theurgic use of the whole Document.

Finally, once a year do this again in a full and concentrated fashion by yourself and in the Circle of Light and watch for new insights, breakthroughs, and spiritual experiences that might flow out of this, and use it as one objective standard of the growth and progress you are making.

10
THE BEATITUDES

Their Nature and Use

The Beatitudes

> Blessed are the poor in spirit: for theirs is the Kingdom of Heaven.
>
> Blessed are they that mourn: for they shall be comforted.
>
> Blessed are the meek: for they shall inherit the Earth.
>
> Blessed are they which do hunger and thirst after righteousness: for they shall be filled.
>
> Blessed are the merciful: for they shall obtain mercy.
>
> Blessed are the pure in heart: for they shall see God.
>
> Blessed are the peacemakers: for they shall be called the children of God.
>
> Blessed are they which are persecuted for righteousness sake: for theirs is the Kingdom of Heaven.
>
> Blessed are ye, when men shall revile you, and shall say all manner of evil against you falsely, for My sake. Rejoice and be exceedingly glad; for great is your reward in Heaven.

The Beatitudes constitute another fundamental pillar of the theoretical and practical training of the Western Spiritual Tradition. Taken as a whole, the Beatitudes embody a blueprint or map for Man's conscious spiritual evolution and the basic guidelines to enable the Candidate to deliberately enter the Path of genuine self-actualization and self-realization in sequential steps.

As with the previous Fundamentals we analyzed, the Beatitudes provide an excellent curriculum or set of materials for us to use the "tools of the trade" and "muscles of consciousness" in the Temple of our Consciousness and Laboratory of our daily lives.

Thus, we can use them alone or in the Circle of Light as our "gymnasium" but always remembering that the true end, or final objective, of all personal and spiritual work, whether done alone or in a group setting, is to embody their underlying spiritual principles in our being and to incarnate or express them in our daily lives.

The fundamental psychological mechanisms and sequential steps that we can use are as follows:

We begin by focusing our attention (or exercising our will through Concentration) upon a selected principle, symbol or idea. Then, we reflect upon it and open our minds to it (or exercise thinking through Meditation).

We continue by looking for personal images or symbols to represent the fruit of our meditation by activating our imagination (or exercising our imagination through Visualization). Simultaneously, we open our heart and pour our emotions into this process (or exercise feeling through Devotion).

The convergence and synthesis of focusing our attention, reflection, the emergence of personal images and symbols, and our love or devotion to them constitute what we have called, in the tradition of Psychosynthesis, Invocation, which may and usually does bring about a consciousness and energy response, an inner awakening, a downpouring or outpouring of Light, Fire and Life which we have called Evocation and which may lead directly to our Contemplation of the principle, symbol, or idea.

When we are really moved and touched emotionally by what we are doing, new attitudes or behavior patterns do emerge which powerfully affect our consciousness and our physical organism by establishing new neural pathways and hormonal responses which then affect our actual behavior. Our behavior, enfleshing or embodying certain principles, ideas, and symbols then transforms our being. When this happens, a feedback loop is then established between consciousness and existence, between willing/thinking and willing/acting, or in other words, between our inner worlds which we are fashioning as their artist, and the outer world in which we live and act. This is what the ancient Sages called "Soul-sculpture" and which constitutes the psychological essence of the Great Work.

This is why Aster Barnwell wrote this concerning the nature and functions of the Beatitudes:

> The Beatitudes can be considered as objective values or outer world equivalents (i.e. in expression) of spiritual principles or laws. As such, their embodiment as part of one's character provides points of contact between one's conscious self and the inner world of principles. As you try to embody the spiritual principles implied by the Beatitudes, you first have to arrive at a *feeling level* as to what the Beatitudes imply in a *practical everyday setting.* This is really the key to the entire exercise. Second, you try to see what practical adjustments you have to make in your personal life in order to establish some resonance (i.e. empathetic

link) with the spiritual principles you are trying to embody. Let me give an example. If you are trying to incorporate the principle of Peace as part of your normal expression, you have to be alert to opportunities to restore harmony out of chaos in the various departments of your life. Instead of thinking of Peace as just the absence of conflict, you yourself have to become a *living* example, an embodiment, a state of Peace.*

The Beatitudes are composed of nine basic affirmations which embody fundamental spiritual Principles or Laws that we have to understand and incorporate in our being and express in our daily lives. These are:

1. **Blessed are the poor in spirit: for theirs is the kingdom of heaven.**

This formula, sung or recited antiphonically, represents, as do later ones, the dialogue between the Higher Self and the lower self, and in so doing, it blazes open a channel between the Superconscious and the Conscious through which we gain the understanding, desire and strength to live them in our daily lives and incorporate them in our character.

> *Blessed:* to bless means to establish a consciousness and energy channel whereby higher energies and vibrations can flow into the lower ones, and the lower ones can harmonize and tune into the higher ones.

> *Poor in Spirit:* to feel a lack of, and a desire for *something* that one feels is very important.

> *Kingdom of Heaven:* is the higher state of consciousness in which Spiritual Consciousness is operating and wherein one experiences one's true Self, God's Wisdom, Love, and Life and the Goodness of Creation.

We can now look at this affirmation as meaning: those

---

*Aster Barnwell, *The Meaning of Christ for our Age*. St. Paul, MN, Llewellyn Publications, 1984, pp. 203-204.

who feel a great lack of and desire for *spiritual things*, which are now perceived as being very important, will eventually be blessed by the Divine Spark, as they seek them, and attempt to embody them and live them.

Vibrate and intone theurgically within your consciousness the following affirmation:

Blessed are the poor in Spirit: for theirs is the Kingdom of Heaven.

What meanings, correspondences, and applications for this formula do you get at this point?

What images and experiences does it evoke for you?

What transformations of Consciousness, energy, and behavior unfold in your consciousness and being?

Use the Consciousness Checklist as an inner, psychological measuring device and ask your friends if they notice any changes in you.

Make sure you record all of this information accurately as soon as possible after you have lived it theurgically and write in your diary how you perceive, define, and respond to the basic events of your life during the period of time you are seeking to unfold new attitudes and behavior patterns that are in harmony with the principles you are working with.

2. **Blessed are they that mourn: for they shall be comforted.**

   They That Mourn: are those who are seeking actively what they feel is very important to them, which they feel they are lacking but which they desire intensely and which provides a very strong growth or transformation impulse.

> ***They Shall Be Comforted:*** means that, eventually, they
> will find that which they seek: they will be blessed
> by the Divine Spark and will attain spiritual Con-
> sciousness which is the Kingdom of Heaven.
>
> In terms of the "Prism" of the Head, Heart, and
> Will, it is useful to remember that it is the Head or
> mind that seeks ... Knowledge, the Heart or
> feelings that ask ... for Love, and the Will that
> knocks or strives for ... Self-expression and Life!
> And that all three facets of the Human Prism are
> activated and fed by Spiritual Energies: Light for
> the Head, Fire for the Heart, and Life for the Will.

This second formula tells us that to achieve Illumination and Spiritual Consciousness, one must "mourn" for it,
that is, desire it intensely, involve one's emotions with it
which will bring down blessings from the Divine Spark and
eventually Spiritual Initiation, which is the only thing that
can bring true and lasting comfort and joy to a human
being.

As such, this affirmation continues and reinforces the
operation begun with the first Petition.

Vibrate and intone theurgically within your consciousness the following affirmation:

Blessed are they that mourn: for they shall be comforted.

What meanings, correspondences, and applications
for this formula do you get at this point?

What images and experiences does it evoke for you?

What transformations of Consciousness, energy, and
behavior unfold in your consciousness and being?

Use the Consciousness Checklist as an inner, psychological measuring device and ask your friends if they
notice any changes in you.

Make sure you record all of this information accurately as soon as possible after you have lived it theurgically and write in your diary how you perceive, define, and respond to the basic events of your life during this period of time you are seeking to unfold new attitudes and behavior patterns that are in harmony with the principles you are working with.

3. Blessed are the Meek: for they shall inherit the Earth.

Meek: esoterically speaking, this does not refer to those who are passive, timid, or cowardly, nor those who will not fight for their self-respect and rights. Rather, in this context, the meek indicate those who are open, receptive to, and making room for the Light, for the flow of Intuition and Inspiration, for the guidance that comes from above and who will not block it off or resist it no matter what the price they may temporarily have to pay for this in the world.

The Earth: refers, on the one hand, to our normal state of consciousness, and on the other hand, to our physical body, our personality or the "Little Kingdom."

This whole formula implies that those who are open and receptive to the Spiritual Energies, and accept the Will of God (of the Divine Spark within) will "inherit the Earth," that is, achieve a psychosynthesis around the center of their Higher Self and acquire self-knowledge and self-mastery.

It also points to the fact that there is a time to face whatever forces confront us and a time to bend to them so as to husband one's resources to be used again at a later time; for the tree that bends to the wind will not be broken, while the tree that does not bend might be uprooted.

Vibrate and intone theurgically within your consciousness the following affirmation:

Blessed are the meek, for they shall inherit the Earth.

What meanings, correspondences, and applications for this formula do you get at this point?

What images and experiences does it evoke for you?

What transformations of Consciousness, energy, and behavior unfold in your consciousness and being?

Use the Consciousness Checklist as an inner, psychological measuring device and ask your friends if they notice any changes in you.

Make sure you record all of this information accurately as soon as possible after you have lived it theurgically and write in your diary how you perceive, define, and respond to the basic events of your life during the period of time you are seeking to unfold new attitudes and behavior patterns that are in harmony with the principles you are working with.

4. Blessed are They which do Hunger and Thirst after Righteousness: for They shall be Filled.

This formula reminds us that those who seek will eventually find what they are seeking, irrespective of how long and hard the search might be. It also reminds us that we must desire righteousness, the Will of the divine in us, as much as we hunger and thirst after food and water, if we are to make true spiritual progress.

Finally, it tells us that to be filled with Divine Light, Fire, and Life, with the Spiritual Energies of the Self, we must desire them and hunger for them with all our heart and soul.

Vibrate and intone theurgically within your consciousness the following affirmation:

Blessed are they which do hunger and thirst after Righteousness: for they shall be filled.

What meanings, correspondences, and applications for this formula do you get at this point?

What images and experiences does it evoke for you?

What transformations of Consciousness, energy, and behavior unfold in your consciousness and being?

Use the Consciousness Checklist as an inner, psychological measuring device and ask your friends if they notice any changes in you.

Make sure you record all of this information accurately as soon as possible after you have lived it theurgically and write in your diary how you perceive, define, and respond to the basic events of your life during the period of time you are seeking to unfold new attitudes and behavior patterns that are in harmony with the principles you are working with.

5. Blessed are the Merciful: for they shall obtain mercy.

This affirmation, whose central symbol is "Mercy" can be interpreted from two basic standpoints: that of the *microcosm* and that of the *macrocosm*.

From the standpoint of the macrocosm, it points to Man's relationship with the world and shows that as one treats others, so will one be treated by them; that if one shows mercy (tolerance, understanding, and compassion) towards others, so in turn, will one be treated with mercy. Underpinning this relationship stands the Law of Action and Reaction (Cause and Effect) or what is known in the East as the Law of Karma.

From the standpoint of the microcosm, it points to the

relationship of Man's conscious with the Superconscious. Mercy is the title and key attribute of *Chesed*, and Chesed is the highest of Man's existential Sephiroth or psycho-spiritual Centers, which connects him with the Supernals. Underpinning this relationship is the Law of Attraction and that in order to "make Gold" one must "have Gold." As the Candidate cultivates and expresses Mercy (tolerance, understanding, and compassion) so will the Higher Spiritual Energies flow from his Superconscious into his consciousness.

As Man gives to his fellow men, so he will receive from the Divine Spark; as the Candidate deals with other human beings on the horizontal dimension so will his inner psychic structure enable the Divine Spark to deal with him.

Vibrate and intone theurgically within your consciousness the following affirmation:

Blessed are the Merciful: for they shall obtain mercy.

What meanings, correspondences, and applications for this formula do you get at this point?

What images and experiences does it evoke for you?

What transformations of Consciousness, energy, and behavior unfold in your consciousness and being?

Use the Consciousness Checklist as an inner, psychological measuring device and ask your friends if they notice any changes in you.

Make sure you record all of this information accurately as soon as possible after you have lived it theurgically and write in your diary how you perceive, define, and respond to the basic events of your life during the period of time you are seeking to unfold new attitudes and behavior patterns that are in harmony with the principles you are working with.

6. **Blessed are the Pure in Heart: for they shall see God.**

The pure in Heart has several meanings and correspondences on different levels of consciousness. The major ones are:

a. To have a Heart Center that is cleansed, awakened, and balanced.

b. To have an Aura that has been cleansed, balanced, and vivified by the Light, Fire and Life of the Divine Spark.

c. To have noble, pure, elevating emotions, desires, and aspirations to love and yearn after the Spiritual Energies—Justice, Goodness, Beauty, and Wholesomeness.

To see God can also have several meanings, chief of which are:

a. To become aware of and experience the Divine Presence, the Light, Fire, and Life of the Divine Spark.

b. To feel and experience the Divine Light, Fire, and Life rushing into our consciousness, quickening and awakening to a larger and higher consciousness.

c. To perceive and experience the Divine Light, Fire and Life in ourselves and in others as our Divine Spark becomes conscious of Itself in our Human Temple.

This affirmation is designed to guide the Candidate to examine, purify and raise his motives, intentions, and aspirations so that by purifying his emotions and intentions, he may enable the Spiritual Energies to flow into his consciousness revealing God's Will to him and quickening him into a new and higher state of being.

Purity is an essential quality and virtue which has profound implications and several aspects at the physical, human, and spiritual levels. Thus there is purity, or the lack of it, at the level of nutrition, breathing, and hygiene (Physical Level); at the level of desiring, feeling, and aspiring as well as in our sexual and love life (Emotional Level); and finally in our psychic and spiritual Lives: energies, vibrations and materials that are drawn into and circulated in our Aura and Tree of Life.

Vibrate and intone theurgically within your consciousness the following affirmation:

Blessed are the Pure in Heart: for they shall see God.

What meanings, correspondences, and applications for this formula do you get at this point?

What images and experiences does it evoke for you?

What transformations of Consciousness, energy, and behavior unfold in your consciousness and being?

Use the Consciousness Checklist as an inner, psychological measuring device and ask your friends if they notice any changes in you.

Make sure you record all of this information accurately as soon as possible after you have lived it theurgically and write in your diary how you perceive, define, and respond to the basic events of your life during the period of time you are seeking to unfold new attitudes and behavior patterns that are in harmony with the principles you are working with.

7. **Blessed are the Peacemakers: for they shall be called the Children of God.**

Peacemakers: we can interpret this symbol horizontally in the world or the macrocosm, and vertically, in Man or the microcosm.

Horizontally, a Peacemaker is a person who helps to settle conflicts and disputes between human beings and who thus facilitates social peace or social integration.

Vertically, a Peacemaker is a person who brings Peace or harmony in his own Psyche, that is, one who strives to achieve his own psychosynthesis. It is also a person who works to harmonize his human faculties with the Divine Will and Life emerging from the Higher States of consciousness, that is a person who strives for union with God, or Spiritual Psychosynthesis.

As a whole, this formula points to the fact that those who strive for Peace, for personal, interpersonal, and transpersonal psychosynthesis will be blessed—that is receive an outpouring of Spiritual Energies from the Divine Spark.

Vibrate and intone theurgically within your consciousness the following affirmation:

Blessed are the peacemakers: for they shall be called the Children of God.

What meanings, correspondences, and applications for this formula do you get at this point?

What images and experiences does it evoke for you?

What transformations of Consciousness, energy, and behavior unfold in your consciousness and being?

Use the Consciousness Checklist as an inner, psychological measuring device and ask your friends if they notice any changes in you.

Make sure you record all of this information accurately as soon as possible after you have lived it theurgically and write in your diary how you perceive, define, and respond to the basic events of your life during the period of time you are seeking to unfold new attitudes and behavior patterns that are in harmony with the principles you are working with.

8. **Blessed are they which are persecuted for righteousness sake: for theirs is the Kingdom of Heaven.**

To be persecuted for Righteousness sake means to be willing to suffer, to undergo hardships, and persecutions for the sake of doing what one knows to be right. Moreover, it requires a great deal of *faith* and conviction in what one knows to be right. Finally, it demands a great effort of the Will which further develops and strengthens the Will.

Unless a person has the courage and strength to fight and suffer for his convictions for what he believes to be right, then he is not ready for and will not be able to implement the promptings of his Divine Spark and higher conscience.

This set of all important faculties or resources:

Faith
Courage
Conviction
Willingness to take risks
Willpower

must be developed on the Path of personal growth and transformation before Illumination can be attained. Once they are developed, and when one is *willing* and *able* to follow the dictates of one's higher conscience (regardless of the personal implications these may have for one's social and material well-being in the world) one will find oneself well on the way to Spiritual Illumination, provided this is the highest ideal and goal one has set for oneself.

Two basic hints can be given for this formula:

1. In order to speed up one's evolution and pay one's

Karmic debts as one is treading the Path of spiritual growth, persecutions and trials of all sorts are most likely to befall the Candidate.

2. That society and social conscience being what they are, it is hardly possible to live in this world and obey the dictates of one's higher conscience, rather than those of society, without being misunderstood and persecuted or ridiculed. But, for those who are spiritually enlightened or well on that Path, persecutions and afflictions have their *raison d'etre* and perform a very useful function in God's Plan.

Vibrate and intone theurgically within your consciousness the following affirmation:

Blessed are they which are persecuted for righteousness sake: for theirs is the Kingdom of Heaven.

What meanings, correspondences, and applications for this formula do you get at this point?

What images and experiences does it evoke for you?

What transformations of Consciousness, energy, and behavior unfold in your consciousness and being?

Use the Consciousness Checklist as an inner, psychological measuring device and ask your friends if they notice any changes in you.

Make sure you record all of this information accurately as soon as possible after you have lived it theurgically and write in your diary how you perceive, define, and respond to the basic events of your life during the period of time you are seeking to unfold new attitudes and behavior patterns that are in harmony with the principles you are working with.

9. **Blessed are Ye when men shall revile you and shall
   say all manner of evil against you falsely for My
   sake. Rejoice and be exceedingly glad; for great is
   your reward in Heaven.**

As suggested in the previous explanation, when a Candidate enters the spiritual Path and begins to tread firmly,
he or she leaves the large and winding road of evolution
that most people travel on for a much narrower and steeper
Path wherein he or she will meet fewer souls. In so doing
two basic things can be expected:

1. The Candidate will have trials, tests, hardships,
   and tribulations that will seem to fall upon him
   from all sides and without respite. He will com-
   press and live through in a shorter period of time
   the experiences and lessons he would normally
   have undergone over a much longer period of
   time. He will greatly accelerate the paying up of
   past Karma and will be tempted and tested way
   beyond what most men and women are.

2. His values, frame of reference, and basic principles will change noticeably, first in his human
   consciousness but also in his overt behavior. Rather
   than living by the values and dictates of his society,
   of what is expedient, rather than pleasing his
   superiors or public opinion, he will do what his
   conscience, what the voice of his Higher Self
   prompts him to do regardless of personal and
   social consequences. Naturally, in so doing, he
   will incur the displeasure, the misunderstanding,
   and the persecutions of many.

If, indeed, it is the voice of his higher conscience, of his
Divine Spark, the Christ within, and not the voice of his
pride, of his reason, or some other subconscious or socio-
cultural entity he is following and suffering for, then two

things will normally ensue:

    a. He will greatly strengthen and further develop his faith, his determination, and his will power.

    b. Once his tests and ordeals in the world are over, he will rapidly expand his consciousness, unfold Spiritual Consciousness, and obtain his reward, which is the bliss and ectsasy of being consciously linked with the Source and Essence of all Wisdom, Love, and Life.

It is well-known that society (the collective conscience of a group) fears and attacks the unfamiliar—those who do not conform to its standards and norms.

Thus, two opposite types of deviants are always persecuted, reviled, and outcast by society: those who are further ahead in evolution, the Saints, Seers and Prophets; and those who are behind in evolution, the criminal, the idiots, and the insane.

Vibrate and intone theurgically within your consciousness the following affirmation:

Blessed are Ye when men shall revile you and shall say all manner of evil against you falsely for My sake. Rejoice and be exceedingly glad; for great is your reward in Heaven.

What meanings, correspondences, and applications for this formula do you get at this point?

What images and experiences does it evoke for you?

What transformations of Consciousness, energy, and behavior unfold in your consciousness and being?

Use the Consciousness Checklist as an inner, psychological measuring device and ask your friends if they notice any changes in you.

Make sure you record all of this information accurately

as soon as possible after you have lived it theurgically and write in your diary how you perceive, define, and respond to the basic events of your life during the period of time you are seeking to unfold new attitudes and behavior patterns that are in harmony with the principles you are working with.

11
THE TEN COMMANDMENTS

Their Nature and Use

The Ten Commandments

1. I am the Lord thy God, thou shall have no other gods before Me.
2. Thou shall not make idols of Me nor bow down to worship and serve them.
3. Thou shall not use the name of the Lord thy God in vain.
4. Thou shall keep holy the day of the Lord thy God.
5. Thou shall honor thy Father and thy Mother.
6. Thou shall not kill.
7. Thou shall not commit adultery.
8. Thou shall not steal
9. Thou shall not bear false witness.
10. Thou shall not covet the wife or any of the possessions of thy neighbor.

From the spiritual and practical viewpoint, the Ten Commandments can be seen as an open and symbolic system with different meanings, correspondences, and applications which change and broaden with our degree of maturity and *lived* experiences, and particularly, with the expansion of our consciousness. As such, the Ten Commandments contain lessons, treasures, and mysteries for persons on all levels of consciousness and evolution, from the lowest to the highest.

The esoteric interpretation of the Ten Commandments that we have developed and lived focuses primarily upon an explanation and application of their Principles and laws to the microcosm, to Man's "Little Kingdom," rather than the macrocosm, to the world. Moreover, this interpretation approaches the Ten Commandments not only as a set of ethical and philosophical guidelines to regulate personal and social behavior, but also as a set of spiritual exercises designed to bring about the completion and perfection of human nature; that is, a psychospiritual transformation through which these Principles can be properly understood and lived in one's daily life. As such, these spiritual exercises require the proper and coordinated utilization of the "tools of the trade" and of the "muscles of human consciousness," the awakening of the human Aura and the activation of the Psychospiritual Centers, and the proper application of Concentration, Meditation, Contemplation, and Theurgy.

These Ten Commandments were given to Moses, the archetype of the mature Candidate or Initiate, on top of Mount Sinai (which is a symbol for the Superconscious) indicating to us that it is only when we reach those levels and are able to reach the heights of the Superconscious that we will truly be able to understand their deeper meanings and applications, and be able to live them in our lives and to enflesh them.

As the Candidate approaches his or her work on the Ten Commandments while using them as a set of practical spiritual exercises and Principles designed to lead to conscious union with God, let the Candidate bear in mind the

Spiritual admonition:
> "If thou wilt enter into the consciousness of Life
> Eternal, keep the Commandments, practice them,
> live them, realize them in thyself, and *become
> them.*"

Then, let the Candidate stand erect, be relaxed, and face
East, vibrating the affirmation:
> "Be silent and know that I am the Lord Thy God."
> or, "Know ye not that ye are the Temple of the
> Living God and that the spirit of God dwells in
> you?"

Finally, let the Candidate bear in mind and reflect
upon the following statements which represent the esoteric
foundation of the Ten Commandments:

a. The Ten Commandments are a set of synthetic formulae containing the symbolic and analogical representation of the Cosmic Laws and Principles
   which order and govern all levels of Being from
   the Spirit (God) to Nature (the physical universe),
   culminating in Man (Humanity).

b. The Ten Commandments embody ever-expanding meanings, correspondences, and applications
   that unfold with the expansion of our consciousness and being, both within ourselves (at
   the subjective level) and in the world (at the objective level).

c. The Ten Commandments can be looked upon as
   containing two fundamental elements: the *Letter,*
   or symbol, which is human, culture-bound, and
   relative to the time, place, and people who produced them; and the *Spirit,* or consciousness and
   energy, which animates and interprets them, and
   which is universal, infinite, and an "open stream of

life and inspiration." Therefore, the central task of the Candidate is to connect the letter or symbols of the Ten Commandments with their spirit through an expanding and maturing consciousness.

d. The Ten Commandments also contain a science and an art; in other words, a theoretical framework and set of guidelines to be applied to one's being and daily life, and a set of practical exercises to activate, cleanse, and coordinate the various psychospiritual Centers of the Tree of Life.

e. In essence, the Ten Commandments embody the Law or Principles that govern the psychospiritual Centers, or "Roses," on the Tree of Life. As such, they constitute the very quintessence of all religious and ethical systems; they order and equilibrate all Worlds and Planes of Consciousness, determining their activities and interrelations from Spirit to Matter. These Ten Commandments will accompany the Candidate step by step on the Path, from his very entrance to it to its very end, when he will have harmonized and integrated his Whole Nature with their spirit. At that point they will be enscribed in "Letters of Fire" in his own heart and they will have become an organized part of his being and life, and his passport to Spiritual Life and Life Eternal.

I. I am the Lord thy God, thou shalt have no other gods before Me.

I am: refers to Man's Divine Spark, or spiritual Self.
Thou shalt have no other gods before Me: implies that no other principle or entity in Man's being, other

than the Divine Spark or the small voice within should become his Center, or the integrating and unifying principle of his Psyche and Life.

In Man's being and life there are presently many principles and entities which do become temporarily his "God" or synthesizing Center. These Gods or synthesizing principles can be:

> his body with its instincts and sensations;
>
> his emotions and strong passions;
>
> his mind and powerful ideas
>
> the major social roles he plays in society, with which he generally identifies;
>
> the living or historical model of another human being;
>
> or even his mystical experiences.

I am the Lord thy God, thou shalt have no other gods before Me.

By vibrating and affirming this Commandment in *Kether*, the Head Center, the Candidate temporarily identifies with his spiritual Self the Divine Spark within, and thereby affirms Its rulership in his being and life in all their dimensions and aspects. It affirms, in other words, "Let the Divine Spark in me be my true Self and rule my being!"

This first Commandment sums up the whole program of spiritual development; it shows the Candidate what he must accomplish while here on Earth and to enflesh this principle so as to gradually bring about his condition on a *permanent basis*—union with the spiritual Self and His rulership in our Little Kingdom; and in our daily life.

Vibrate and intone this formula inwardly and/or outwardly and see what happens . . .

What meanings, correspondences, and applications do you get at this point? What images and experiences do they evoke for you? What transformations of conscious-

ness, energy and behavior do they bring about in your consciousness and being? Use the Consciousness Checklist as
an inner, psychological measuring device and ask your
friends if they notice any basic changes in you.

Make sure that you record all this material accurately
as soon as you have *lived it theurgically* and write down in
your diary how you perceive, define, and respond to your
Self and to the basic events of your life during the period of
time you are working with this affirmation.

I am:

The Lord thy God:

No other gods before Me:

II. Thou shalt not make idols of Me nor bow down to worship and serve them.

> *Idols:* the key symbol of this Commandment is the
> word "Idol" that comes from the Greek word
> *eidolon* which means images or thoughtforms.

This Commandment organically continues the process set in motion by the first Commandment. It is not
enough to affirm that it is the spiritual Self rather than the

many human selves of a person that he should identify with and establish as the Center, or unifying principle, of his being and life, for there is a basic difference between the spiritual Self, His Life and Consciousness and the many possible mental representations and symbols that a person can create about the spiritual Self during his long evolutionary journey.

This Commandment stresses the basic difference between "Form" and "Force," between a mental representation and a living reality. In order for consciousness to formulate and express itself, it needs the twin polarities of form and force, and Man must, of necessity, use symbols and representations of Higher Beings, Realities, and states of consciousness, but he can be aware of what they are: a means to an end, and not the end in itself, and thus not confuse them with the reality for which they stand.

For a human being, the ultimate form or vehicle (called a "Temple" by the various religious traditions) is the Psyche, the human Aura, and the Tree of Life, and not a mental or a material representation of it.

Man has created countless idols or images of the spiritual Self which he has presented in Icons, statues, or words and he has worshipped many "Gods" (money, sex, and power being the most popular ones!) and he will continue doing so, but he can do this being aware of what he is doing and not confusing the image for the reality which it represents.

Thou shalt not make idols of Me nor bow down to worship and serve them.

This Commandment continues the process set in motion by the first Commandment and is designed to help the Candidate differentiate between the Divine Spark Himself and His Life and Consciousness that reside in the upper reaches of human consciousness, and the many mental representations of the Divine Spark (God within).

This affirmation makes possible for the candidate to distinguish between *Creator* and *creation* (between force and form) and to integrate the two in his consciousness.

Vibrated in *Chockmah,* this affirmation enables the Candidate to unfold a true perspective of himself of his fellow Pilgrims, and of God, which is true Wisdom.

Vibrate and intone this formula inwardly and/or outwardly and see what happens . . .

What meanings, correspondences, and applications do you get at this point? What images and experiences do they evoke for you? What transformations of consciousness, energy and behavior do they bring about in your consciousness and being? Use the Consciousness Checklist as an inner, psychological measuring device and ask your friends if they notice any basic changes in you.

Make sure that you record all this material accurately as soon as you have *lived it theurgically* and write down in your diary how you perceive, define, and respond to your Self and to the basic events of your life during the period of time you are working with this affirmation.

Make Idols:

Of Me:

Bow down to worship and serve:

III. Thou shalt not use the name of the Lord thy God in vain.

> *Use the name of God in vain:* exoterically, this means
> to use lightly or irreverently *any* Name of God or
> Word or Power.
>
> Esoterically, however, it implies vastly more.
> The "Name of God" implies His Presence, His
> Consciousness, His Life, and Energies.

This affirmation vibrated in *Binah* means not to abuse
one's being, which is the Temple of the Divine Spark, in any
way—it also means not to misuse or drain one's Energies,
the Light and Life that one receives from on high, or one's
consciousness, thoughts, emotions and desires in such a
way as to cut them off from their central Source, at the One
Reality or the spiritual Self.

Presently human beings abuse themselves and their
energies in countless ways on the physical, emotional and
mental levels. By *not* using the Name of God in vain, the
Candidate can achieve and maintain harmony with his
Divine Spark and become harmless to others . . . and to
himself!

Finally, this affirmation deals with the Mystery of Harm-
lessness to oneself and to others, with the Cultivation of
Reverence for Life and Sensitivity to God's Will and Plans.

Vibrate and intone this formula inwardly and/or outwardly and see what happens . . .

What meanings, correspondences, and applications
do you get at this point? What images and experiences do
they evoke for you? What transformations of consciousness, energy and behavior do they bring about in your consciousness and being? Use the Consciousness Checklist as
an inner, psychological measuring device and ask your

friends if they notice any basic changes in you.

Make sure that you record all this material accurately as soon as you have *lived it theurgically* and write down in your diary how you perceive, define, and respond to your Self and to the basic events of your life during the period of time you are working with this affirmation.

Name of the Lord:

Use in vain:

IV. Thou shall keep holy the day of the Lord thy God.

> *To keep holy:* means to preserve the harmony, the relationship or connectedness that will enable something to remain whole or balanced.
>
> *The day of the Lord:* has several meanings and correspondences, chief of which are: the amount of time dedicated to God or to direct spiritual work, thereby establishing contact with the Divine within, on the vertical axis (from the Heart to the Head Center) through Prayer. It also implies the Spiritual Plane and Spiritual consciousness through which the Divine Spark may be contacted, and the sevenfold cycle of activity in which each phase has its own distinctive characteristics.
>
> *The Lord thy God:* clearly refers to the Divine Spark at the core of one's being.

One of the most important tasks that a human being can accomplish while here on Earth is to create, forge, and fashion his own little world—to bring about a psychosocial cosmos out of the chaos within himself. The creation of Man's own universe involves structuring his space, time, and actions, and this Commandment deals with the proper structuring of Man's time so as to enable it to flow whole, and therefore to live a wholesome life.

The major units of time for Man are the day, the week, the month, and the year; this Commandment draws the Candidate's attention to the fact that during each period of time (a day a week, a month, a year, and even a lifetime) he should periodically set some time aside for focusing his attention to the Divine Within, to actively seek to align his consciousness and life with the Will of the Divine Spark, and to raise his consciousness on the Holy Mountain to the point where he can come into conscious contact with the Living Light and Fire, Love and Consciousness, of the Divine Within.

Here, the key is to keep a proper balance and rhythm between work, prayer, and relaxation, between his physical, human, and spiritual activities, and between his professional, personal, and spiritual life, thereby to tune into the various parts of his being and of the world which are material, psychic, and spiritual in nature.

This affirmation, in other words, deals with the Mystery of Growth and Rhythm, and with the proper structuring of time. It focuses the Candidate's attention upon *Chesed* which is the highest Psychospiritual Center that Man can activate while incarnate on Earth, and which represents Chronos or Time, called by the Greeks "the Father of Gods."

Vibrate and intone this formula inwardly and/or outwardly and see what happens . . .

What meanings, correspondences, and applications

do you get at this point? What images and experiences do they evoke for you? What transformations of consciousness, energy and behavior do they bring about in your consciousness and being? Use the Consciousness Checklist as an inner, psychological measuring device and ask your friends if they notice any basic changes in you.

Make sure that you record all this material accurately as soon as you have *lived it theurgically* and write down in your diary how you perceive, define, and respond to your Self and to the basic events of your life during the period of time you are working with this affirmation.

To keep holy:

The day of the Lord:

The Lord thy God:

V. Thou shall honor thy Father and thy Mother.

> *Thou:* refers to the human self, the conscious rational ego acting within the Field of Consciousness.
> *Honor:* a. To become aware of, to focus one's attention upon.
> b. To enter into a proper relationship with.
> c. To give and receive what is due.

Father: a. The Spirit Which is both within Man and in the World (God and the Divine Spark Which are One in Essence).

b. The active, dynamic Male Principle which operates both in Man's being and in his life; in what he *is* and what he *does*.

Mother: a. Nature, the physical plane which is both in Man (his body) and in the World (the physical world).

b. The passive, receptive Female Principle, which operates both in Man's being and in his life, in what he *is* and what he *does*.

Let us look at this petition as a whole, keeping in mind the symbolism and images asociated with each Word of Power:

1. We become aware that man is *both* Spirit and Matter as is the whole world, and that we must enter into a proper relationship with the Divine Spark and the body, and with God and Nature in the world. Furthermore, we must abide by the Laws of the Spirit and Nature—to give God what is His "due" and the World what is its due, in other words to realize that one has both spiritual needs and aspirations as well as physical needs and aspirations.

2. We become aware that man is *both* Male and Female, and there are times when one should act in a dynamic way, affirming one's ideas and will, and times when one should act in a passive way, receiving and accepting what comes to one in life.

3. Finally, this Petition means for us to become aware of and to synthesize properly the myriad of masculine and feminine forces, energies, and polarities which constitute and mold our being, existence, and becoming:

subjective — objective
prayer — work
knowledge — love
severity — mercy
grace — effort
asceticism — joie de vivre
joy — pain
spirit — matter
good — evil
accepting one's fate — struggling
    against fate.

This Commandment focuses upon *Geburah,* awakening it and connecting it with *Chesed,* thereby synthesizing their principles and energies. It is this Affirmation which deals with the Mystery of Polarity and the realization of synthesis on many levels.

Vibrate and intone this formula inwardly and/or outwardly and see what happens . . .

What meanings, correspondences, and applications do you get at this point? What images and experiences do they evoke for you? What transformations of consciousness, energy and behavior do they bring about in your consciousness and being? Use the Consciousness Checklist as an inner, psychological measuring device and ask your friends if they notice any basic changes in you.

Make sure that you record all this material accurately as soon as you have *lived it theurgically* and write it down in your diary and how you perceive, define, and respond to your Self and to the basic events of your life during the period of time you are working with this affirmation.

Thou shall honor:

Mother:

Father:

VI. Thou shalt not kill.

This Commandment implies not to destroy that which exists before its natural time for disintegration has come, be it a human being, a creature, an intuition, thought, feeling, aspiration, belief, word or deed. It is the principle which deals with reverence for life both generically and specifically. It means, essentially, not to create disharmonies, not to interfere with what exists, both inside oneself as well as outside of oneself, by the imposition of one's will and ideas, but instead to fulfill one's role, mission, and place in life according to God's will and thus to consciously harmonize one's self with the Divine Spark and Its Plan of Evolution.

This Affirmation also deals with unfolding the feminine, receptive, harmonizing principle within one's self and in one's life. It is linked with *Tiphareth* and activates its energies and principles, synthesizing within itself all that descends from above and all that ascends from below. For example, to suffocate someone with affection is just as much a violation of this Commandment as it would be starving someone's emotional needs with too much austerity. It is at this level that the true synthesis of *Chesed* and *Geburah* (mercy and severity, spirit and matter, male and female) is truly realized within one's being and life, at the level of *Tiphareth* when the latter is properly activated.

Vibrate and intone this formula inwardly and/or outwardly and see what happens . . .

What meanings, correspondences, and applications do you get at this point? What images and experiences do they evoke for you? What transformations of consciousness, energy and behavior do they bring about in your consciousness and being? Use the Consciousness Checklist as an inner, psychological measuring device and ask your friends if they notice any basic changes in you.

Make sure that you record all this material accurately as soon as you have *lived it theurgically* and write down in your diary how you perceive, define, and respond to your Self and to the basic events of your life during the period of time you are working with this affirmation.

Kill:

VII. Thou shall not commit adultery.

From the esoteric viewpoint Adultery means to lose the state of *purity and clearness,* concentration and integration that one possesses. It implies to split or dissociate the Psyche from some of its functions, components and energies. This can occur by desiring, wanting, or willing the wrong thing (or the right thing at the wrong time).

Adultery also means that one should not unite, mate, incorporate, or establish a "circuit" (take into one's Aura or link one's Aura) with the being, energy, or entity which is not for you, or which is not in your path of evolution. Properly understood and lived by, it leads one to unite and mate, on all levels, only according to God's Will as this Will becomes manifest in your being and life. To give the reader a practical example, to do something only because it is practical, desirable, or expedient are all instances of committing adultery.

This commandment also links one's conscious ego with *Netzach*, activating it and purifying it (or polluting it when it is violated). It deals with the the Mystery of Desire, wanting and willing on the conscious, concrete level.

To want what is wrong brings dissociation, confusion, and misery in its wake, whereas to want what is right brings synthesis, clarity, peace, certainty and joy as its natural consequence.

Vibrate and intone this formula inwardly and/or outwardly and see what happens . . .

What meanings, correspondences, and applications do you get at this point? What images and experiences do they evoke for you? What transformations of consciousness, energy and behavior do they bring about in your consciousness and being? Use the Consciousness Checklist as an inner, psychological measuring device and ask your friends if they notice any basic changes in you.

Make sure that you record all this material accurately as soon as you have *lived it theurgically* and write down in your diary how you perceive, define, and respond to your Self and to the basic events of your life during the period of time you are working with this affirmation.

Commit Adultery:

VIII. Thou shall not steal.

This Commandment tells us plainly that we should not take what does not belong to us, whether this is a physical, emotional, mental or spiritual thing; whether it be a person, an energy, or an object, and appropriate it to oneself.

It implies to *know* and to *take* only that which God sends to us for our good and growth, and not to use our will and resources to arbitrarily get what we want at the moment.

It also means to grow consciously and in harmony with the Will of the Divine Spark (and therefore, with our self, society, and nature) without either forcing or hindering its growth.

This Commandment focuses on *Hod* and activates it, and it also balances and connects *Hod* and its energies and principles with the energies and principles of *Netzach*. It deals with the Mystery of not wanting and doing what is not for you, but to align your conscious ego with the Will and Energies of the Spiritual Self to bring about a true harmony and growth at the personality level in your being and in your life.

Vibrate and intone this formula inwardly and/or outwardly and see what happens . . .

What meanings, correspondences, and applications do you get at this point? What images and experiences do they evoke for you? What transformations of consciousness, energy and behavior do they bring about in your consciousness and being? Use the Consciousness Checklist as an inner, psychological measuring device and ask your friends if they notice any basic changes in you.

Make sure that you record all this material accurately as soon as you have *lived it theurgically* and write down in your diary how you perceive, define, and respond to your Self and to the basic events of your life during the period of time you are working with this affirmation.

Steal:

IX. Thou shall not bear false Witness.

To bear false Witness means either to affirm that which does not correspond to reality or to project a thoughtform that is not anchored in life, a process which creates a dissociation within the Psyche and which will, eventually, be revealed for what it is.

This Commandment also implies not thinking, feeling, saying, or acting things which one knows are false.

Finally, it urges that one does not destroy the image of things by adding or cutting, magnifying or diminishing the reality of things. In essence, it implies not creating any thoughtforms which are contrary to the Will of the Divine Spark, not to congest and confuse one's mind, emotions, and social relations with wishful thinking or fanciful emotions.

This Commandment focuses on *Yesod*, activating it, cleansing it, and bringing it into proper alignment with the Higher Centers and with *Malkuth*. Thus it enables the Candidate to preserve a healthy equilibrium between ideals and reality, theory and practice, individual freedom and social constraints; and, on another level, this Commandment enables us to speak to each in his own language and to adapt to one's socio-cultural environment; that is, in the language of the Mystery Tradition "to wear the clothes of the country one finds oneself in."

Vibrate and intone this formula inwardly and/or outwardly and see what happens . . .

What meanings, correspondences, and applications do you get at this point? What images and experiences do they evoke for you? What transformations of consciousness, energy and behavior do they bring about in your consciousness and being? Use the Consciousness Checklist as an inner, psychological measuring device and ask your friends if they notice any basic changes in you.

Make sure that you record all this material accurately as soon as you have *lived it theurgically* and write down in your diary how you perceive, define, and respond to your Self and to the basic events of your life during the period of time you are working with this affirmation.

Bear false Witness:

X. Thou shalt not covet the wife or any of the possessions of thy neighbor.

This is the only Commandment which applies fully and literally to the material Plane, as it deals with *Malkuth*, activating it, cleansing it, and equilibrating it. It also complements the seventh Commandment on the physical Plane as the latter deals with the psychological Plane and the motivational dimension.

In essence this Commandment means: you will not desire to receive, be, or become anything but what you are, have, and can become according to the Will and Plan of the Divine Spark. It implies that if you see something someone else has that you will not desire it, or be it, without working for it and creating it by your own efforts, once you have obtained the confirmation from the voice within that you are doing the right thing.

If you violate this Commandment, as we often do, what you would get would not be yours, organic to your being, but external to you, and a burden for your human and spiritual unfoldment. And, it would probably generate social conflict and bring about a struggle with others who want to preserve what they have.

Finally, it also means to not to want to evolve too quickly or too slowly, but to wait for the right moment and the natural unfolding of your faculties, energies, joys, and experiences.

To give, desire, or accept gifts indiscriminately is violating this Commandment. The "wife of thy neighbor" is not only his woman but also his faculties and Female Principle. The "possessions of thy neighbor" are not only what he has and owns but also what he *is* and what he has *achieved.*

Vibrate and intone this formula inwardly and/or outwardly and see what happens . . .

What meanings, correspondences, and applications do you get at this point? What images and experiences do they evoke for you? What transformations of consciousness, energy and behavior do they bring about in your consciousness and being? Use the Consciousness Checklist as an inner, psychological measuring device and ask your friends if they notice any basic changes in you.

Make sure that you record all this material accurately as soon as you have *lived it theurgically* and write down in your diary how you perceive, define, and respond to your Self and to the basic events of your life during the period of time you are working with this affirmation.

Covet the wife:

Possessions:

Thy Neighbor:

All of these Commandments, Laws, and Principles prepare the Candidate, by degrees, to achieve the incarnation of the Word or the proper alignment of his human self (from within the center of the Field of Consciousness) with his spiritual Self (in the Superconscious) and to receive an inflow of Light, Fire, and Life that can permeate his whole being and touch every Center and Plane.

Thus, the whole Tree is touched and affected, and every Principle in Man is nourished and aligned with the Divine Spark. Man can grow and mature only through *action*, through the use of all the faculties and energies of human nature and which make right human relationships possible. The "Great Chain of Being" and the inner link and harmony are thus preserved from the Divine to the physical Plane of Being.

Furthermore, the Ten Commandments have an inner threefold manifestation:

1. The first subdivision deals with the Spirit, or the spiritual Self, and Its conscious realization.
2. The second, third, and fourth deal respectively with the manifestation of the spiritual Light, Fire, and Life in Creation; with preserving the proper alignment, harmony, and flow between the Divine Spark and the various Planes of Creation, both

within Man and outside of his being.

3.   The fifth to the tenth deal, essentially, with the sphere of the right human relationships, and with the preservation of the proper harmony in one's interpersonal relationships so that the Light, the Fire, and the Life of the Divine Spark can flow, unimpeded and undistorted, through one's Tree of Life to others and from others to oneself in an unbroken fashion.

At this point, you might want to use other perspectives and sets of meanings to interpret and make the Ten Commandments come alive for you and reveal further Mysteries and Treasures. For example, you might want to take the framework of Psychosynthesis, or even develop your own personalized system, to see what theoretical insights and practical exercises might be revealed to you so that you can enflesh them in your own being and life. Thus, the first Commandment points to spiritual Psychosynthesis and to Self-identification: making the spiritual Self the true Center and unifying principle of your Psyche. The second, third, and fourth Commandments point to personal Psychosynthesis and to the Principle of Disidentification and proper energy handling. Finally, the fifth to the tenth Commandment point to interpersonal Psychosynthesis and the Principle of right human relationships.

The two Royal Commandments of the New Testament.

If the Ten Commandments were the cornerstone of the Old Testament, the two Commandments given by Jesus are the cornerstone of the New Testament, and in fact, the *synthesis of all Commandments,* the very foundation of any type of genuine Spiritual work. These two Commandments are:

1. **Thou shalt love the Lord thy God with all thy heart, all thy soul, and with all thy mind . . .**
2. **And thy fellow men as thyself.**

These two Commandments depict symbolically the interrelationship between the Trinity (Father, Son, and Holy Spirit; Wisdom, Love, and Will; God, Man, and Nature; the Spiritual, the Psychic, and the Physical Planes; and the Spiritual Energies manifesting as Light, Fire and Life) and Duality (God and Man; Spirit and Matter; and Male and Female).

As such, they indicate to the Candidate how he can consciously cooperate in his becoming, in the fashioning and forging of his being, and in the realization of his perfection. Thus they deal with the Mysteries of the Trinity and of Duality with their ever-expanding meanings, correspondences, and applications on the different Levels of consciousness and Planes of being.

Man, who is an objectified and manifested emanation of the Trinity (that is, who is a triune being: Spiritual, psychic, and physical; the being in whom force and form express as consciousness, and the being whose central attributes and needs are Wisdom, Love and Life) *is a Microcosm of the Macrocosm!* This means that he has his being and operates both in the outer, or objective world, and in the inner, or subjective world, and is thus also a dual being. As such, he must grow and expand both inwardly and outwardly.

What flows into Man from the higher reaches of his Psyche, he must manifest in the world. This is the philosophical foundation of the Great Work, and it is the cognitive handle by which to make Faith and Ritual come alive and become effective.

Vibrate and intone this formula inwardly and/or outwardly and see what happens to you.

What meanings, correspondences, and applications do you get for these Commandments? What images and experiences do they evoke for you? What transformations of consciousness, energy and behavior do they bring about in your consciousness and being? Use the Consciousness Checklist as an inner, psychological measuring device and ask your friends if they notice any basic changes in you.

Make sure that you record all this material accurately as soon as you have lived it theurgically and write down in your diary the results you obtained from this "inner work."

Thou shall love the Lord thy God with all thy heart, all thy soul, and with all thy mind:

And thy fellow men as thyself:

Use each of the Ten Commandments for your inner and outer work (consciousness expansion and transformation and behavioral changes) for the period of one month. With the remaining two months of the year, you can use the whole Document simultaneously. Each year, take one month to go over the entire Document carefully, recording the new insights, exercises, and transformations that have occurred as you grow and unfold your consciousness and level of being.

12
THE HAIL MARY

Its Nature and Use

The Hail Mary:
The Mother of the Lord and Light-giver, let us exalt:
Hail O Birth-giver Mary, full of grace, the Lord is with Thee.
Blessed are Thou amongst women and blessed is the fruit of Thy womb.
For Thou hast borne the Savior of our Souls.

The Hail Mary is the Christian version of a most important Document of the *Hagia Sophia*, the Ageless Wisdom, which has its functional equivalents in many different religious and spiritual traditions.

Short and simple as it may appear, it is a most important formula embodying profound esoteric knowledge and an integrated series of practical exercises designed to establish a breakthrough of the Superconscious into the Conscious, to fill the human Aura with spiritual Light, Fire, and Life, to activate and awaken key psychospiritual Centers on the Tree of Life, and to harmonize the human self with the Spiritual Self culminating in genuine spiritual Illumination—the dawning of Spiritual Consciousness.

All the psychospiritual work that the candidate has done so far: developing the tools of the trade, training the muscles of consciousness, visualizing, cleansing, and consecrating the human Aura, activating and lighting up the psychospiritual centers on the Tree of Life, and working with the other Fundamentals through the four phases of Concentration, Meditation, Contemplation, and Theurgical expression, can now be focused upon and culminate in living and becoming the Hail Mary. The ultimate objective and achievement for the Candidate with this Petition is to *become the Theotokus, the birth-giver of God* (as the Eastern Orthodox calls the Virgin Mary).

In the microcosm (that is, in Man) the Theotokus, the Mother of the Lord and Light-giver is his own soul, his Consciousness, Aura, and Tree of Life, whence the Light flows and which must at some point, become the "Birth-giver" or "matrix" for the Christ-consciousness.

In the macrocosm (that is, in the World) it is the *Anima Mundi*, the Soul of the world, or the Earth's collective psychospiritual atmosphere.

In history, Mary (the Mother of the Master Jesus) became the archetype or perfect symbol and personification of the human soul and the *Anima Mundi*. She was considered an advanced Initiate Who became the earthly Mother of the Man in Whom the Christ Spirit would incarnate fully and consciously. Therefore, Mary represents the Ideal Woman, the reflection of the Female Principle and the incarnation of the Eternal Feminine—a part of which we all have within our being.

To exalt the Light giver means to focus all our attention, thoughts, feelings, and energies upon our Soul and Tree of Life, in order to raise its vibratory rate and to heighten our state of consciousness so that it wil become a Light and Life Giver, the seat of the Christ-Consciousness, for ourselves and for the world.

Hail O Birth-Giver Mary, Full of Grace, the Lord is with Thee.

This affirmation contains one of the most powerful

spiritual exercises the Candidate can use to fill his soul with Light, to raise his vibratory level, and to expand his consicousness. As with all other spiritual exercises, it demands Faith to make it "operational," that is, we need to have the ability to concentrate, to meditate, to visualize, to open one's Heart, to have a practical understanding of what one is doing and why, and a profound Love for God and for the Great Work.

Hail O Birth-Giver Mary: here the Candidate focuses his consciousness upon his Soul, reminding himself and then experiencing that his Soul is the "Birth-giver" or matrix for human consciousness on all Planes of Being, and that it is in his own Tree of Life that, for him, God, Man, and Nature are "born" (spring forth into consciousness).

Full of Grace: the Candidate now visualizes and experiences the Divine Light, Fire, and Life slowly filling his entire Aura, activating his Tree of Life, and suffusing his whole consciousness.

When performed with the utmost Faith (and when the Candidate is ready for it) this is the exercise that will bring about the "Golden Dawn" of spiritual Consciousness, the slow awakening of a higher and qualitatively different state of consciousness in him.

The Lord is with Thee: by concluding with this affirmation the Candidate affirms and should experience that once his Soul, Aura, and Tree of Life have been purified and consecrated by the Divine Light, the Divine Spark can then consciously operate through it.

This operation contains and represents the Great Work in its essence and the ultimate realization that all human beings must eventually come to and experience the Union of God with Man, of the Spiritual Self with the Psyche so that human consciousness can now manifest and reflect Spirit in matter.

Vibrate and intone this formula inwardly and/or outwardly and see what happens . . .

Hail O Birth Giver Mary, Full of Grace, the Lord is with Thee.

What meanings, correspondences, and applications do you get at this point? What images and experiences do they evoke for you? What transformations of consciousness, energy and behavior do they bring about in your consciousness and being? Use the Consciousness Checklist as an inner, psychological measuring device and ask your friends if they notice any basic changes in you.

Make sure that you record all this material accurately as soon as you have *lived it theurgically* and write down in your diary how you perceive, define, and respond to your Self and to the basic events of your life during the period of time you are working with the affirmation.

Hail O Birth Giver Mary:

Full of Grace

The Lord is with Thee:

Blessed are Thou amongst women and Blessed is the Fruit of Thy Womb.

> *Blessed amongst Women:* has two meanings (or one meaning on two levels):
> a. That the woman, or human being, who succeeds in establishing a breakthrough, or a conscious contact with the Divine Spark, will be blessed. This means to *experience a transfer of life, energy and consciousness from a higher source to a lower one,* in this case from the spiritual Self into the human self and its vehicle of expression—the Psyche.
> b. That the Feminine Principle which succeeds in establishing a contact and rapport with the Divine Spark, will likewise, be Blessed and enlivened.

> *Blessed is the Fruit of Thy Womb:* means that the Being or Principle to which the woman (or the Feminine Principle) is giving birth is also Blessed.

Every woman and every Feminine Principle must give birth to some "Being" or Principle. Love (if it is genuine) must and will bear "fruit," but this fruit can appear on different Planes of Being. It can be a child on the physical Plane, but it can also be a feeling, an idea, an intuition, a new insight, realization, or state of consciousness.

A Female Principle without love will remain barren, and a barren Female Principle will always remain an unfulfilled Female Principle. Whatever is "born" always reflects the nature and origin of the Male and Female Principles that gave birth to it, the "Force" and the "Form" which engendered it. In this case, what is "born" (the Fruit) is Spiritual

Consciousness, which is engendered by the spiritual Self and by the Psyche, which is now in contact with the Divine Spark Which Blesses His Offspring in human consciousness.

Vibrate and intone this formula inwardly and/or outwardly and see what happens . . .

Blessed are thou amongst women and blessed is the fruit of Thy womb.

What meanings, correspondences, and applications do you get at this point? What images and experiences do they evoke for you? What transformations of consciousness, energy and behavior do they bring about in your consciousness and being? Use the Consciousness Checklist as an inner, psychological measuring device and ask your friends if they notice any basic changes in you.

Make sure that you record all this material accurately as soon as you have *lived it Theurgically* and write down in your diary how you perceive, define, and respond to your Self and to the basic events of your life during the period of time you are working with this affirmation.

Blessed amongst Women:

Blessed is the fruit of Thy womb:

For Thou hast borne the Saviour of our Souls.

This affirmation further reinforces and completes the preceding one. Exoterically, the Savior of our Soul is Jesus Christ.

Esoterically, however, it is the Divine Spark which engenders true Spiritual Consciousness in the Tree of Life and in human consciousness.

This last affirmation now completes the whole transformational process. At this point, the Candidate should feel and experience that his Soul is filled with Divine Light, Fire, and Life, that his consciousness is in direct contact with the Spiritual Self, and that he has been "saved."

Vibrate and intone this formula inwardly and/or outwardly and see what happens . . .

For Thou hast borne the Saviour of our souls.

What meanings, correspondences, and applications do you get at this point? What images and experiences do they evoke for you? What transformations of consciousness, energy and behavior do they bring about in your consciousness and being? Use the Consciousness Checklist as an inner, psychological measuring device and ask your friends if they notice any basic changes in you.

Make sure that you record all this material accurately as soon as you have lived it Theurgically and write down in your diary how you perceive, define, and respond to your Self and to the basic events of your life during the period of time you are working with this affirmation.

For Thou hast borne:

The Saviour of our Souls:

There are other meanings and exercises attached to the Hail Mary and which the Candidate can find in various traditions such as Psychosynthesis and the Qabalah. These are all useful provided they are properly understood, regularly practiced, and finally *lived* and *enfleshed*.

The Candidate should bear in mind a most important point: if he or she has diligently and regularly practiced the work and exercises that we proposed and described in this work, having arrived at this point, and particularly with the mastery and incarnation of the Hail Mary, the Candidate should have attained an authentic degree of Spiritual Consciousness, a breakthrough of the Superconscious into the Conscious, and an attunement of the human with the Spiritual Self. When this has *experientially occurred*, regardless of what specific Path or system has been used to "get there" (and these are many), the candidate will now have aligned his consciousness with a LIVING SOURCE OF KNOWLEDGE AND GUIDANCE WITHIN HIMSELF or HERSELF! which will then render all external guides, paths, and systems obsolete. From that point onwards, he or she will *be the path* and the Supreme Initiator will be his or her own Divine Spark.

It used to be said that all roads led to Rome or Jerusalem. The same could be said of the various religions, metaphysical, esoteric or spiritual Paths and Systems, for like the spokes of a wheel, they all converge upon the same center. Once one has attained this center, it makes little difference what Path one has traveled to get there, and one can then reorganize the usefulness and validity of all genuine Paths and systems which are always means, but never the true end . . . which is God Himself.

Let the candidate work on the four affirmations of the Hail Mary, taking one each week, and then dedicating a full month to Theurgic Work on the whole Document.

Finally, at the end of each new year (and of the previous work he has recapitulated for that year) let the Candidate complete his "spiritual retreat" or Meditations, Contemplations, and Theurgic Invocation with that of the Hail Mary . . . until he or she becomes the Living Theotokus, the Birth-giver of God, at which point it will be the Christ-Child, or Consciousness, Who will continue and complete the Great Work of spiritual Illumination and Initiation about which only silence and the direct, personally lived *experience* of the Candidate can be the Revealer and Teacher.

13
CONCLUSION

*The Nature and Use of your own personal
Energy, Consciousness, and Light Generator,
Transformer, and Amplifier*

Today, you and I are privileged to be alive in a very interesting age, the distinctive feature of which is a massive and accelerated *psychocultural transformation,* a transition from one state of being and consciousness to another, from one world to another. Thus, we are all spectators and actors in a great crisis, both internal (bio-psycho-spiritual) and external (social, political, and cultural).

It is interesting to note and reflect upon the fact that the Chinese have two basic characters to denote a crisis, one indicating great danger, and the other great opportunities, and it is these two fundamental traits that best characterize our being and our world at the present time.

The greatest challenge, both personal and collective, that we are all facing and involved in, will be discussed at length and analyzed in full details in another forthcoming work*; the essence of this challenge can easily be represented by two simple yet complex words: **danger** and **opportunity**.

The danger is that we can *degenerate* and extinguish civilization and the very life of our planet, while the opportunity is that we will *regenerate* ourselves, enter into a

---

*Apocalypse Now, Llewellyn Publications

New Age which entails basically a new state of consciousness and being, and a new lifestyle. These imply taking a very radical and fundamental quantum leap forward in our evolution, wherein humanity will finally enter its adult or mature period when we will know who we are, where we are going, and what we are meant to achieve in this Earthly, material existence. They also imply becoming the masters of our being, of our lives, and of our destiny, and then becoming integrated and whole beings who have integrity and act in a responsible fashion in all of Creation.

This is what has been described in the language of the Sacred Traditions as "entering the Promised Land" where a new Heaven (a new state of consciousness and level of being) and a new Earth (lifestyle, culture, and world) await us. This is also the passage from the 5th Root Race to the 6th Root Race which will give birth to the New Man, the Son of Man, forseen and prophesied by Jesus and by so many Prophets and Seers both old and modern. Finally, this is what will make us the 10th Hierarchy in the Great Chain of Being that stretches from Spirit to Matter so that both personally and collectively we will be able to be and act as God's Energy and Consciousness Transformers for the Divine Light, Fire and Life of God. In order for this to happen, we must all become consciously and actively involved in the real drama of human *becoming.* We must all, personally and collectively, engage in what has very aptly been called "Soul Sculpture" or becoming the Artists of our Consciousness, Being, and Lives, and acting as the central interface or transducers between Spirit and Matter. This is why the pioneers of unknown continents and lands and later the astronauts of the solar system must now become the "endonauts" and "psychonauts" of the inner universe of life and consciousness.

To properly accomplish this Great Task we need a

new and integral Philosophy and Art of Living as well as practical and effective technologies of consciousness and energy transformation. We need a new cognitive framework and practical psychospiritual exercise that represent the simple and effective synthesis of the Sacred Traditions of the Past with the very best of the modern social sciences, the fusion of theory and practice, and the proper blend of idealism with realism. And all of this expressed in simple, practical, and effective language and illustrations that are meaningful to, and workable for, the average man and woman of good will.

This is what I perceive to be the fundamental challenge of our time and the greatest need of our age. Thus, it is to respond in a positive, constructive fashion to this fundamental challenge and to answer in a creative way this great need that the Llewellyn Spiritual Sciences series was born, and that *The Nature and Use of Ritual for Spiritual Attainment* and *The Invisible Temple* were written and published. In these two works the essence of this Integral Philosophy of Life and Art of Living is presented in a simple, practical, and effective fashion for you, the reader, to understand and be able to live the Yoga of the West, the quintessence of our own spiritual Tradition and the contemporary flowering of the very best of our modern social sciences, so as to enable you to bridge the Sacred and the Profane, the Esoteric with the Exoteric dimensions of our cultural heritage.

Our emphasis in *The Nature and Use of Ritual for Spiritual Attainment* has been on the cognitive aspect of this Great Work, and in *The Invisible Temple* on the practical aspects. Remember that theory and practice must always come together to be truly alive and fruitful, and that knowledge which is acquired for curiosity's sake or for ego aggrandisement and which is not *lived*, in the end always turns into "poison" (a burden, confusion, or a hindrance to true living). In these works we have taken some of the most important Prayers and Rituals of the Chrisitan Tradition, which is one expression of the Timeless and Universal Wisdom of Humanity, to analyze and decode them from the perspective of the esoteric or Spiritual Traditions which can be found both in History and Personal Experience. These have yielded a rich crop of psychospiritual techniques and exercises that constitute the essence of the present work. But, as with the Yoga of the East, or any Yoga for that matter, let the reader bear in mind and meditate upon the fact that it is not the techniques or the practical exercises *per se* that are truly important and the heart of this Great Work. Useful and needed as these techniques and exercises may be and are, they are but the outer garment of the true body of the Great Work.

Saints, Sages, and true Masters of both the East and West have never tired of warning their followers and disciples that it is not the siddhis (the psychospiritual powers and exercises) that are the main object and aim of this work and adventure; rather, that it is the conversion, the expansion and transformation of Consciousness and Being, "living the Life," as the Ancient Christians called it, knowing and doing the will of God, of the True Self, and especially loving God, Humanity, and Nature (which naturally implies loving ourself) with all our *heart, mind,* and *soul,* which constitutes the true heart and substance, the very foundation and body of the Great Work.

This truly cannot be said enough times or emphasized enough for most seekers and New Age Persons are far more concerned with having more and more of what the Ego wants, and not what the Self wants; concerned more with health, wealth, and love and greater personal power than with true holiness and the practice and the embodiment of the virtues—Justice, Beauty, Truth, Goodness, and Purity.

In the authentic spiritual Quest, authenticated by all

the genuine Masters of Humanity and by the teachings of the great world Religions, and of all valid esoteric Orders, what is sought as the grand and culminating objective of all striving and personal work is *Union with God*—to know the Self and offer Him a properly coordinated and organized personality as His Temple in the material world so that His Will may be manifested in Creation Consciously.

This union with God brings a shifting of identity and of the center of our being from the *human* to the *spiritual* Self yielding Peace of Mind, serenity, and a clear Conscience, the ability to face constructively whatever experience and tests life may bring, and the ability to respond to His Promptings and Guidance in an adequate and effective fashion. It also brings Balance between our physical, emotional, mental, and spiritual nature, states of consciousness, energies, faculties and activities which is also the true meaning of the Greek "Harmony" which the Christians called "the Peace Profound that passeth human understanding." As the reader can readily see, this is very different from expanding our consciousness and heightening our energies so as to develop clairvoyance, telepathy, psychokinesis, out-of-the-body experiences, ecstasies and visions, or gaining an edge over others and being able to control and manipulate them for our own personal interests and goals!

There is a fine line between psychic development and spiritual awakening, between developing our personality and empowering our human will and surrendering them to the Self, and there is a right time and way to do both!

In Psychosynthesis the integration of these polarities is called respectively *self-actualization* and *self-realization*, and the former must precede and then be integrated with the latter.

Self-actualization actually implies the full development and coordination of the personality and its various faculties and "muscles": willing and Concentration, thinking and Meditation, feeling and Devotion, imagination and Visualization, Intuition and Invocation/Evocation, bio-psychic drives and Energy Transformation and Direction, and sensation and Inner and Outer Observation; as well as the proper development and mastery of our physical, emotional, and mental nature, and the professional roles we play in the world and which give us power and status in our society.

Self-realization, on the other hand, implies the discovery, attunement, and integration with the Self and the offering of our personality, our will, consciousness, energies, and resources to the Self so that He may utilize them for his ends and objectives. This also involves the fundamental dichotomy between *egoism*, which is a preliminary means, and *altruism*, working and living for the whole, which is the true end.

There is nothing wrong, and in fact it is our duty to develop a healthy well-balanced, and effective personality and a sharply honed will, but we must ever bear in mind that, when we have achieved this, it is only to offer them to the Higher Self and not the human ego.

This raises another very important point: the deepest and most powerful and universal yearning and striving of human beings have always been and still are those for knowledge, love, and power, for the development and full expression of the Head, the Heart, and the Will. But these must always be balanced and properly synthesized, for too much Knowledge, or Love, or Power, can, by themselves, become demonic, or lead to a fundamental unbalance, and to what theology calls "Sin," particularly the achievement of Power without Wisdom and Love to use it properly and lovingly for the Whole! It is precisely this situation which now confronts us squarely in the face. Ever since the Renaissance and particularly since the Age of Reason, humanity has embarked on an express train to gain more and more

Knowledge leading to personal power over Nature and over others, while neglecting Wisdom and especially Love.

Today, what Humanity needs is not more Knowledge or more Power, or bigger machines, or better technologies, but more selfless, altruistic love—the ability to establish right human relationships with ourselves, with others, with Nature, and with God. This is what we must unfold and express if we are to survive the present World Crisis and enter the New Age. At the same time, this is what stands at the very heart and soul of the Great Work and of the Yoga or Philosophy and Art of Living we are presenting to you:

The ability to love ourselves, God, Humanity, and Nature with all our hearts, minds, and will— the ability to unfold and live right relationships with the whole!

This is what the serious Candidate should ever bear in mind, meditate upon, and seek to enflesh from the very beginning to the end of the Path.

A final but most important point is the understanding and realization of a proper synthesis of Introversion/Extroversion, Supraversion/Infraversion, and of the Male/Female Polarities for therein lies the true key to balance, harmony, or peace, just as the Psyche is the key to unlock the Mysteries of the Universe and of Life.

By the proper use of the perspective and tools that have been suggested in this work, the Candidate should meditate upon, seek to reconcile and finally live the opposed psychological tendencies of directing his or her energies and attention upon the outer and inner worlds, upon the spiritual and the physical aspects of his or her being, and of being active and self-affirming or passive and receptive. Finally, Idealism should also be tempered and reconciled with Realism so that one moves not too fast yet not too slowly either in one's growth, self-actualization and self-realization.

To properly understand and work with the Yoga of the West (the nature and use of Symbols and Rituals) it is very important to plan and organize one's life and activities so as to live consciously and in a responsible and effective fashion. To this end, it is fundamental to learn to work alone, with one's Guides, with one's Brothers and Sisters on the Path, and with the Community at large.

It is equally important to learn proper self-observation and monitoring by keeping an accurate and regular diary and workbook wherein one will record the work and exercises one has done, when they were accomplished, and under what conditions and with what results; also to be recorded is the state and unfoldment of one's consciousness, life, and being: what we do in our daily lives, what happens to us, and how we perceive, define and respond to both what we have done and to what has happened to us.

Finally, it is crucial that the Candidate organize a proper time, place, and state of conditions to do the work in a serious and effective fashion.

At which point, the Candidate is now ready to reread this Workbook and absorb its overall perspective, central insights, and basic tools and exercises to gain a good intellectual grasp of the work it suggests. He should carefully reflect and meditate upon exactly what he or she wishes to personally accomplish, how much time, energy, and resources he is willing to allocate to this great adventure of personal psychospiritual transformation, what changes and adjustments might be required of him in his or her daily life, attitudes, and relationships, and then develop a practical plan of action for daily, weekly, and monthly work.

In this age of anxiety, uncertainty and of overchoice coming from competing systems, approaches, and ever proliferating options, it is vital that the Candidate chooses one to three basic ideas and exercises, that he practices them daily to develop the functions of the Psyche which I have termed the "muscles of human consciousness," and that he prepares the outer and inner Temple and Sanctuary where the actual work will be done.

Rather than experimenting lightly and for a short period of time with various Fundamentals and exercises that might sustain his interest and feed his curiosity, it is far preferable to concentrate upon a few essential tools and techniques to make sure that these are properly understood and ready to be lived and then to begin the actual work on an appropriate date.

In the Great Work of personal psychospiritual transformation and spiritual awakening, the Candidate works essentially with three distinct entities which he must know and have mastered properly. These are: the basic Tools of the Trade, Master Rituals, and Himself and his consciousness. The tools of the trade which can be exercised, developed and refined by using the Master rituals or other exercises are:

    a. The "muscles of human consciousness" or the seven functions of the Psyche with their related psychospiritual exercises:

        Willing and Concentration
        Thinking and Meditation
        Feeling and Devotion
        Imagination and Visualization
        Intuition and Invocation-Evocation
        Biopsychic Drives and Energy
            Transformation and Direction
        Sensations and Outer and Inner

Observation

b. The four stages of personal transformation, consciousness expansion, and spiritual awakening:
    Concentration
    Meditation
    Contemplation
    Theurgy

c. The four phases of the growth process, self-actualization and self-realization:
    Thinking and Knowing
    Feeling and Desiring or Loving
    Willing and Acting
    Living and Becoming

The Master Rituals as described in this work are:
Divine Names: Their nature and proper use.
The Sign of the Cross: its nature and proper use.
The Lord's Prayer: its nature and proper use.
The Nicene Creed: its nature and proper use.
The Beatitudes: its nature and proper use.
The Ten Commandments: its nature and proper use.
The Hail Mary: its nature and proper use.

Finally, Man and his consciousness involve the following elements:
a. The four basic Auras or energy-fields of the Candidate: the Etheric, Astral, Mental, and Spiritual.

b. The Tree of Life and its ten Psychospiritual Centers: *Kether, Chockmah, Binah, Chesed, Geburah, Tiphareth, Netzach, Hod, Yesod* and *Malkuth* operating in the four Worlds:

> Atziluth — the Divine World
> Briah — the Superconscious
> Yetzirah — the Conscious
> Assiah — the Subconscious
> > and Unconscious

c. The Inner and Outer Temples and their Sanctuary: the Psyche with Its Auras and Tree of Life and the Physical Temples with their Sanctuaries and symbols, colors and paraphernalia.

d. The Inner (vertical) and Outer (horizontal) Generator-Circles in his Aura and in the Physical world.

All of the Tools of the Trade, the Master Rituals, and the Consciousness of the Candidate are used synergistically in what I have called the "Energy, Light, and Consciousness Generator, Transformer, and Amplifier" (or the Outer and Inner Circle of Light) which is the *grand synthetic exercise* suggested by the work.

With proper and regular use of the Circle-Generator, the Candidate will find both personal healing and enlightenment, fundamental insights and guidance, the central and growing motivation and the energies and resources necessary to bring about psychospiritual transformation and growth. Within it, a "feedback loop" is established such that the candidate will be able to train and unfold the "Tools of the Trade," unveil and experience the Mysteries and Treasures of the Master Rituals, and enliven and transform his Consciousness.

While the opening Phase of the Circle-Generator is basically "closed" and structured so as to ensure the proper

"balancing" and "recharging or energizing" of his Phys-
ical-Etheric, Astral, Mental, and possibly also of his Spiritual
vehicles, which will be brought into proper alignment, the
Closing Phase of the Circle-Generator is open-ended and
self-unfolding, leading to ever deepening and heightening
realizations and experiences.

Herein lies the true passage from the Outer to the
Inner Temple of the Mysteries, from the elementary to the
advanced Work, and from the human to the spiritual Self.

In our present personal and world crisis the Circle of
Light Generator could well become your most valuable
asset and investment, and your personal "Noah's Ark," giving you shelter, healing, and life from the Outer and Inner "storms."

It is recommended that it be used to that end, giving
the best of yourself to it, so that you may truly make it your
own and then be able to offer it to the World . . . and to
God.

"In order to make Gold, one must have Gold" declares
an old Alchemical axiom which means that before the Candidate can operate seriously and effectively with the Master
Rituals and with Himself and his consciousness, he must
have trained, developed, and refined his Tools of the Trade
to a certain extent . . . that is, that he has developed a true
devotion and dedication to the Great Work, that he has an
"operational" faith and that he has a genuine reverence for
Life and Love, for God, and for his fellow human beings.
Then, and only then, can he practice and live the four basic
injunctions of the Esoteric Schools:

TO KNOW
TO DARE
TO DO
TO BE SILENT

and then to invoke the Higher Energies and States of Consciousness to descend upon him and to suffuse his being in

a safe, balanced, and practical fashion.

It is also of vital importance that he understands that he is, himself, the ultimate crucible, or laboratory, for all experiments and discoveries which must be tested out in his daily life.

When working with Symbols, Rituals, and Sacred Myths, the Candidate must find out for himself or herself what specific and personalized meanings and applications these have for him at this point in his life and in his development, and in his present state of consciousness. Thus he must ask himself over and over again as he proceeds on the Path and in the process of personal psychospiritual transformation:

a. What meanings, correspondences, and practical applications do these have for him *now*?

b. What transformation of consciousness, energy, and behavior do they unfold in his consciousness and being *now*?

c. What Theurgic impact do they have upon his consciousness, Aura, and Tree of Life *now*?

d. The Candidate must use the Consciousness Checklist as an inner, psychological measuring device and ask his friends if they notice any changes in him, in his life, behavior, and relationships *now*.

e. Finally, he must record faithfully in his workbook what he has done, when, under what conditions, and with what results and write accurately in his diary how he now perceives, defines and responds to the basic events of his life during the period of time he is working with these Symbols, Rituals and Myths.

Lastly, the Candidate must watch carefully and monitor his own growth and development so that he will be aware of and sensitive to the great moment when his intuition will become operative, when the Spiritual Consciousness will dawn in him, and when the Christ-child will be born in the "Manger" of his own Heart. For, at that point, he will become a truly autonomous being, guided from within, rather than from without, and these Symbols, Rituals, and Myths will finally become truly dynamic and alive in him revealing their own deeper mysteries and treasures. For then the Candidate will have become a genuine Priest and Initiate and thus be able to do unique and irreplaceable work in the world to further God's plans and his or her own *becoming* in a synergistic fashion.

Appendix: A

A LETTER TO THE CANDIDATE

During the last 25 years of my life, I have personally tested and retested the basic Philosophy of Life and Art of Living based upon the Seven Fundamentals and the basic approach and exercises described and analyzed in depth in *The Nature and Use of Ritual for Spiritual Attainment* and outlined for their practical use and incorporation in one's daily life in this book.

I have used *myself*, my own Psyche and Consciousness, and my *daily life* with its countless experiences, tests, and adventures as the essential testing ground and laboratory to check out their validity and effectiveness in the modern World. Most of what has been discussed and suggested in these two works, which I consider the most important works of my life, has been unveiled and revealed to me progressively, and on an ongoing basis, by the very Symbols and Rituals I have been using.

What I *am*, what I *know*, and what I *live* today is largely the result of this great spiritual adventure I began early in my life. Moreover, if I am alive, sane, and productive today, it is precisely because I had and used this knowledge which has served me best in the most trying times of my life. I can honestly say that I was able to pass through the greatest and most painful crisis and tests of my life because I *knew* and *lived* this Philosophy and Art of Living which has rightly been called the *Hagia Sophia*, the Holy Wisdom or Ageless Wisdom.

For me, it has indeed proven itself to be an effective Philosopher's Stone capable of transmuting the hardships, sufferings, and ordeals of life into Human and Spiritual Gold—of transforming negative into positive, Evil into Good, and meaninglessness and despair into purpose and hope. Thus, it is from my own being and my own experience that I have gleaned and distilled what is herein offered to you, the reader and Candidate. Finally, these fundamental insights, principles, and perspectives together with their practical exercises and techniques have also been tested and lived by men and women of many generations and belonging to very different times, societies, and cultures, and living under a very different set of personal and collective conditions. They can be found, by those who have eyes to see and ears to hear, in all the great World Religions and Spiritual Traditions of East and West, in the Occult, Mystical, and Magical Traditions as well as in the latest developments of modern social sciences, and ultimately, in the very *consciousness* and Peak Experiences of any dedicated, qualified and trained person. Thus, they are far from being a new philosophy, metaphysical system, or esoteric Cult for they are verified and corroborated both by Tradition and by Personal Experience.

During the last quarter of a century, I have also worked with and trained many individuals and groups who have used themselves and their own personal lives and experiences as the final "laboratory" and "Court of Appeal."

In various degrees and in different and unique ways, every person who has seriously dedicated himself or herself to the process of psychospiritual transformation and spiritual awakening has benefitted from them and grown from this "adventure" which, of all human adventures, is certainly the greatest, the most rewarding, yet the most difficult and most demanding!

Each person has discovered some universal and some unique aspect and result of this work. What has been outlined and suggested in these two works constitute the elementary aspects, or the foundation of the Great Work, the "Entrance of the Path," as it were, for about the intermediary and advanced levels of this Work and Path to self-actualization and self-realization little can be said and written—most of it must be personally *lived, discovered* and *experienced . . .* and *exemplified in silence.*

If the fundamental and overall goals and objectives of this Great Work can be intellectually described and outlined, they would be to:

1. Become more alive in all the aspects and facets of one's being so as to be able to accept, integrate and function in all the Dimensions of Creation—to become whole so as to live a wholesome life (which to me, is the true meaning of "Salvation").

2. To discover, unite with, and become one's true Self so as to be able to manifest this Self and its Attributes of Divine Wisdom, Divine Love, and Divine Creative Energies in as clear and undistorted a fashion as possible.

3. To be able to accept and be grateful for all human experiences with no exceptions and thus to transmute Evil into Good, and thereby, to truly LOVE ONESELF: God, Humanity, and Nature in *all* of their aspects and facets.

4. Finally, to develop a true REVERENCE FOR LIFE by facilitating the conscious expression and manifestation of Life through one's being and life, and those of others.

If the concrete and specific goals and objectives of this

Great Work can be intellectually described and outlined, they would be:

a. To awaken, activate, and coordinate one's intuition so that one can become an autonomous and responsible being with true integrity who is now able to be guided from *within* and to be independent of external authorities, teachers, and books.

b. To learn and live the Yoga of the West which is Theurgy—the use of Symbols and Rituals as Energy and Consciousness Transformers to contact, bring through, and circulate the Divine Light, Fire, and Life of the Divine Spark. To make all Symbols, Myths, and Rituals come alive, speak to us, and reveal their Mysteries and Treasures—our latent Potentials, the higher reaches of our consciousness, and our dormant or "entombed" Divinity.

c. Finally, to be able to consciously and actively participate in the Communion of our human with our Spiritual Self, so as to achieve, at least, a temporary *Union with God.*

But now, dear reader and Candidate, you have heard the Good News and obtained an intellectual glimpse and foretaste of what all valid Religions, Spiritual Traditions, and Philosophical Schools have promised, which I have tried to summarize in its essentials in this workbook. It is up to you to do the work, it is up to you to truly discover, live, and become what all this means, using *yourself:* your being, your life, and your consciousness as the final laboratory and "arbiter."

You must plant these "Seeds" in the "Garden of your Consciousness" and make them grow to see what kinds of Trees and Fruits they will bring to you! You must test and retest, experiment with, and especially *live* these Fundamentals so that they can become alive for you, and speak to you, and transform your being and your consciousness, leading you to the promised land—to a new Heaven and a new Earth, to your true Self and the *fulfillment of your destiny!*

Peter Roche de Coppens Ph.D.
East Stroudsburg University
East Stroudsburg, PA
1985

Appendix: B

VARIOUS DIAGRAMS OF THE TREE OF LIFE AND HUMAN AURA

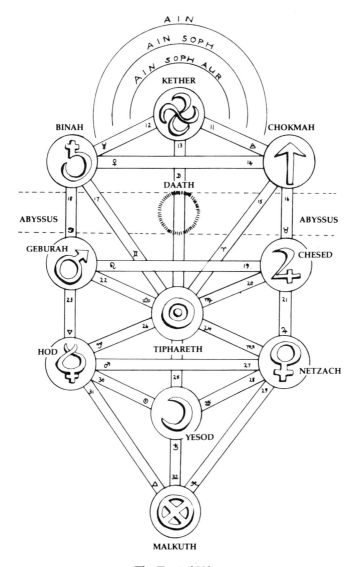

The Tree of Life

Melita Denning & Osborne Phillips, *The Sword and the Serpent*. Llewellyn Publications, 1975.

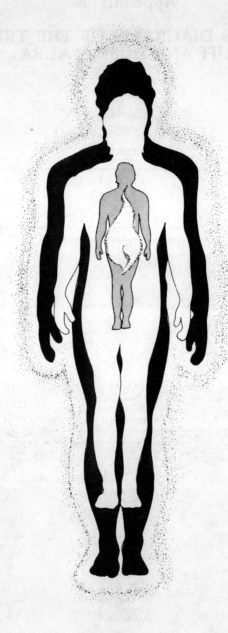

The Human Aura

The Human Aura

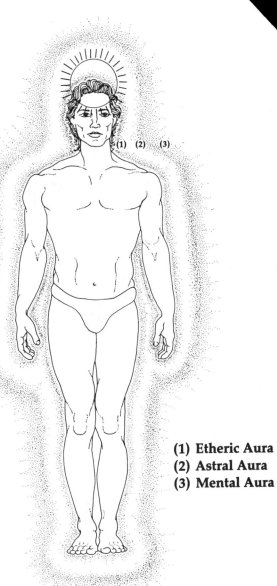

(1) Etheric Aura
(2) Astral Aura
(3) Mental Aura

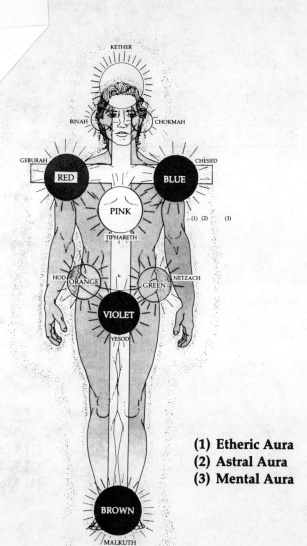

(1) Etheric Aura
(2) Astral Aura
(3) Mental Aura

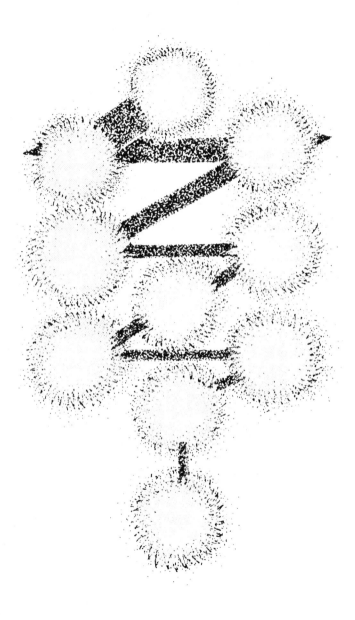

The Flashing Sword

Melita Denning & Osborne Phillips, *The Sword and the Serpent*. Llewellyn Publications, 1975.

The Rising Snake

Israel Regardie, *The Golden Dawn*. Llewellyn Publications, St. Paul, MN. 1984.

Appendix: C

CONSCIOUSNESS CHECKLIST

The Consciousness Checklist described below is a practical instrument we have derived from Roberto Assagioli's *Egg of Psychosynthesis* which represents, diagrammatically, and describes the *structure* of the human Psyche. Its seven basic categories or questions are drawn directly from the Field of Consciousness and its seven functions: Willing, Thinking, Feeling, Intuition, Imagination, Biopsychic Drives, and Sensations. It is a most important psychological tool designed to enable the Candidate to develop his/her capacity for inner observation and to monitor what is really happening in his/her Consciousness, to note and evaluate the qualitative and quantitative changes and psychospiritual transformations that might occur as the result of particular work being done, using Ritual or practicing other psychospiritual exercises.

It is the primary tool, operationalized from Psychosynthesis theory, for self-observation and consciousness-examination we are offering the reader and Candidate. As such, it should be properly memorized and understood in sequential order, and then used before, during and at the end of doing the entire range of individual exercises, Rituals, and the operation of the Circle of Light Generator we are suggesting in this book. Its proper use will enable the Candidate to systematically become aware of his/her inner state, of the processes and materials at work in his/her Field of Consciousness, and of possible transformations that will occur therein. These should then be noted mentally and/or in his/her workbook.

This is a tool that I have used not only for esoteric/spiritual work but also for psychological, human growth, and psychotherapeutic purposes, and which has yielded excellent results. Its merit is to be, at the same time, simple and practical as well as systematic and exhaustive, tapping not only quantitative but also qualitative possible changes.

Consciousness Checklist

1. What *sensations* are you presently aware of in your field of Consciousness?

    a. Seeing

    b. Hearing

    c. Tasting

    d. Smelling

    e. Touching

    What sensations are particularly strong, and which are weak?

Where do these sensations come from?

Realize that you are *not* these sensations, but that they are tools for you to contact the Physical World.

2.   What *biopsychic drives* or *impulses* are you presently aware of in your Field of Consciousness?

       a.   Hunger

       b.   Thirst

       c.   Fatigue

       d.   Sexual Arousal

       e.   Anger or Aggressiveness

3.   What *emotions* and *feelings* are you presently aware of in your Field of Consciousness?

       a.   Joy

       b.   Sorrow

       c.   Love

   d.   Fear

   e.   Excitement

   f.   Depression

   g.   Other

What emotions and feelings are particularly strong, and which are weak? Where do these come from?

Realize that you are *not* these emotions and feelings, but that they are tools for you to use and that *you* control them, that they are not really a part of your true being, but act as a source of great energy and drive, joy or sorrow.

4. What *images* or *symbols* are presently activated in your imagination?

   a.   Natural

   b.   Human

   c.   Spiritual

What images are particularly strong, and which are weak?
Where do these images and symbols come from?

Realize that you are *not* these images and symbols, but that they are tools for you to reproduce the other functions of the Psyche and experiences you have or could live.
Presently, is your image-making function strong or weak?

5. What *thoughts* or *ideas* are presently going through your mind?

    a. Of the Past

    b. Of the Present

    c. Of the Future

What thoughts and ideas are particularly strong, and which are weak?
Where do these thoughts and ideas originate?

Realize that you are *not* these thoughts and ideas, but that they are tools for you to use to express yourself on the Mental level, and that *you* can control them.

6. Is your *intuition* presently active in your Field of Consciousness?

a.   Spiritually

b.   Mentally

c.   Emotionally

d.   Physically

If it is active, what is it telling you?
Does any part of your being oppose or thwart your intuition?
Can you distinguish between your intuition, emotions, imagination, and biopsychic drives?

Realize that you are *not* your intuitions but that these are tools for you to contact the deeper and higher parts of your being and of life.

7.   What are you presently *willing?*

a.   Physical objects

b.   Emotional objects

c.   Mental objects

d.   Spiritual objects

How well can you presently use your will and ability to concentrate upon the above objects? In your outer work and inner work, are you able to do what *you* want and not to do what *you* do not want?

What is preventing you, if anything, from presently using your will efficiently?

How can you develop your will further?

Appendix: D

THE PSYCHOSPIRITUAL CENTERS OF THE TREE OF LIFE AND THEIR MOST IMPORTANT PRACTICAL CORRESPONDENCES

The Psychospiritual Centers, Spheres, or Sephiroth of the Tree of Life have well-established and ever-growing and expanding attributions, correspondences, associations, and practical applications. One of the main contributions of *The Nature and Use of Ritual for Spiritual Attainment* and of the present book is to have linked the Tree of Life with what I called the "Seven Fundamentals" and to have derived new correspondences and practical applications for Meditation and Theurgic living. Here below are summarized those traditional attributions, correspondences, associations, and practical applications of the Tree of Life which are deemed most important for the work suggested, together with their correspondences and practical applications for the Seven Fundamentals.

Please note that both the Nicene Creed and the Hail Mary have no direct correlations with the Ten Spheres. Both could more easily be correlated with some of the Paths that link the Spheres than with the Spheres themselves. The Creed basically unfolds a theology, anthropology, and cosmology describing *in symbols* the biography and action of the Divine Spark in Its journey through the physical world. The Hail Mary, on the other hand, focuses our attention and psychic energies upon our own Aura and Consciousness to fill them with Light so as to bring about the *birth of Spiritual Consciousness* in our Hearts, and to circulate that Light and Consciousness in our being and to radiate them in the world.

Also included are the correlations for the Hierarchies and the Seven Sacraments which can add to our esoteric and kabalistic understanding of the Christian Religion.

KETHER: THE CROWN

Position in the human body: The Head.
Position in the Temple: The Dome, Roof, or Window above the Altar.
Force: Unity.
Functional Color: Pure White Brilliance.
Name of Power: Eheieh, I Am, Father.
Archangel: Metatron.
Angels: Chioth ha Qadesh, Holy Living Creatures.
Planetary Attribution: Primum Mobile, First Swirlings.
Magical Image: An Ancient Bearded King seen in Profile.
Spiritual Experience: Reunion with the Source.
Virtue/Vice: Completion of the Great Work/None.
Titles: Ancient of Days, the White Head, Lux Occulta.
Symbols: The Crown, the Point within a Circle.
Precious Stones: Diamond.
Perfume: Ambergris.
Divine Names: The Father, the Creator, the Source, the Crown.
Sign of the Cross: In the Name of the Father.
Lord's Prayer: Our Father Who art in Heaven.
Beatitudes: Blessed are the poor in spirit . . .

Ten Commandments: I am the Lord Thy God . . .
Hierarchies, Exoteric/Esoteric: Pope, Patriarch/Ipsissimus
(honorary for incarnate beings).
Seven Sacraments: None.

CHOKMAH: WISDOM

Position in the human body: The Left Cheek.
Position in the Temple: Left Frescos, Ikons, Windows
below Dome and behind Altar.
Force: Expansion.
Functional Color: Gray.
Name of Power: Yahveh, Lord, Wisdom.
Archangel: Ratzkiel.
Angels: Auphanim, the Wheels.
Planetary Attribution: Zodiac.
Magical Image: A Bearded Male Figure.
Spiritual Experience: Vision of the Source We Seek.
Virtue/Vice: Devotion/None.
Titles: Power of Yetzirah, Abba, The Supernal father.
Symbols: The Phallus, Yod, The Tower, the Rod.
Precious Stones: Star Ruby.
Perfume: Musk.
Divine Names: Wisdom.
Sign of the Cross: None.
Lord's Prayer: Hallowed be *Thy* Name.
Beatitudes: Blessed are they that mourn . . .
Ten Commandments: Thou shall not make idols of Me . . .
Hierarchies, Exoteric/Esoteric: Cardinals, Metropolitans/
Magus (honorary for incarnate beings).
Seven Sacraments: None.

BINAH: UNDERSTANDING

Position in the human body: The Right Cheek.

Position in the Temple: Right Frescoes, Ikons, Windows below Dome and behind Altar.

Force: Contraction.

Functional Color: Black.

Name of Power: Yahveh Elohim.

Archangel: Tzafkiel.

Angels: Aralim, the Thrones.

Planetary Attribution: Saturn.

Magical Image: A Mature Woman.

Spiritual Experience: Vision of Sorrow.

Virtue/Vice: Silence/Avarice.

Titles: Ama, the dark Sterile Mother; Aima, the bright Fertile Mother; Marah, the Great Sea.

Symbols: The Yoni, the Cup or Chalice.

Precious Stones: Star Sapphire, Pearl.

Perfume: Myrrh, Civet.

Divine Names: Understanding.

Sign of the Cross: None.

Lord's Prayer: Hallowed be Thy *Name*.

Beatitudes: Blessed are the meek . . .

Ten Commandments: Thou shall not use the Name of the Lord Thy God in vain.

Hierarchies, Exoteric/Esoteric: Archbishop/Magister Templi (honorary for incarnate beings).

Seven Sacraments: None.

CHESED: MERCY

Position in the human body: The Left Shoulder.

Position in the Temple: Left Angel, Ikons behind Altar.

Force: Order.

Functional Color: Blue.

Name of Power: El, God.

Archangel: Tzadkiel.

Angels: Chasmalim, the Brilliant Ones.

Planetary Attribution: Jupiter.
Magical Image: A mighty Crowned and Throned King.
Spiritual Experience: Vision of Love.
Virtue/Vice: Obedience/Bigotry, Hypocrisy/Gluttony.
Titles: Gedulah, Love, Majesty, Magnificence.
Symbols: The Scepter, the Wand, the Crook, the Orb.
Precious Stones: Amethyst, Sapphire, Lapis Lazuli.
Perfume: Cedar.
Divine Names: Mercy.
Sign of the Cross: And of the Holy Spirit.
Lord's Prayer: Thy Kingdom Come.
Beatitudes: Blessed are they which do hunger and thirst
    after Righteousness . . .
Ten Commandments: Thou shall keep holy the Day of the
    Lord Thy God.
Hierarchies, Exoteric/Esoteric: Bishop (unconscious)/Adep-
    tus Exemptus (conscious).
Seven Sacraments: Matrimony.

GEBURAH: SEVERITY, MIGHT

Position in the human body: The Right Shoulder.
Position in the Temple: Left Angel, Ikons behind Altar.
Force: Energy.
Functional Color: Red.
Name of Power: Elohim Gebor, Mighty God.
Archangel: Khamael.
Angels: Seraphim, Fiery Serpents.
Planetary Attribution: Mars.
Magical Image: A Mighty Warrior in his Chariot.
Spiritual Experience: Vision of Power.
Virtue/Vice: Energy, Courage/Cruelty, Wanton Destruc-
    tion.
Titles: Pachad, Fear, Justice.
Symbols: The Pentagon, the Sword, the Spear, the

Scourge.

Precious Stones: Ruby.

Perfume: Tobacco.

Divine Names: Severity, Might.

Sign of the Cross: And of the Holy Spirit.

Lord's Prayer: Thy Kingdom Come.

Beatitudes: Blessed are the merciful ...

Ten Commandments: Thou shall honor thy Father and thy Mother.

Hierarchies, Exoteric/Esoteric: Priest (unconscious)/Adeptus Major (conscious).

Seven Sacraments: Holy Orders.

TIPHARETH: BEAUTY, HARMONY

Position in the human body: The Heart.

Position in the Temple: The Altar.

Force: Equilibrium.

Functional Color: Pink.

Name of Power: Yahveh, Eloah Ve Daath, God made Manifest in the Mind.

Archangel: Raphael.

Angels: Malakim, Kings.

Planetary Attribution: The Sun.

Magical Image: A King, a Child, A Sacrificed God.

Spiritual Experience: Vision of the Harmony of Things, Understanding of Sacrifice.

Virtue/Vice: Devotion to the Great Work/False Pride.

Titles: The Lesser Countenance.

Symbols: The Red Cross, the Calvary Cross, the Truncated Pyramid.

Precious Stones: Topaz, Yellow Diamond.

Perfume: Olibanum (Frankincense).

Divine Names: Beauty, Harmony, Christ.

Sign of the Cross: And of the Son.

Lord's Prayer: Give us this Day our Daily Bread.
Beatitudes: Blessed are the pure in heart ...
Ten Commandments: Thou shall not kill ...
Hierarchies, Exoteric/Esoteric: Deacon (unconscious/Adeptus Minor (conscious).
Seven Sacraments: Communion, the Eucharist.

NETZACH: VICTORY

Position in the human body: The Left Hip.
Position in the Temple: Candles on the Altar.
Force: Combination.
Functional Color: Green.
Name of Power: Yahveh Tzabaoth, Lord of Hosts.
Archangel: Haniel.
Angels: Elohim.
Planetary Attribution: Venus.
Magical Image: A beautiful naked Woman.
Spiritual Experience: Vision of Beauty Triumphant.
Virtue/Vice: Unselfishness/Unchastity, Lust for Power.
Titles: Firmness, Valor, Triumph.
Symbols: The Lamp, the Girdle, the Rose.
Precious Stones: Emerald.
Perfume: Rose, Red Sandalwood.
Divine Names: Victory.
Sign of the Cross: None.
Lord's Prayer: Forgive us our trespasses as we forgive those who trespass against us.
Beatitudes: Blessed are the peacemakers ...
Ten Commandments: Thou shall not commit adultery.
Hierarchies, Exoteric/Esoteric: Subdeacon (unconscious)/ Philosophicus (conscious).
Seven Sacraments: Absolution.

HOD: SPLENDOR, GLORY

Position in the human body: The Right Hip.
Position in the Temple: Book, Bible on the Altar, the Lectern or Pulpit.
Force: Separation.
Functional Color: Orange.
Name of Power: Elohim Tzabaoth, God of Hosts.
Archangel: Michael.
Angels: Beni Elohim, Children of God.
Planetary Attribution: Mercury.
Magical Image: A Hermaphrodite.
Spiritual Experience: Vision of Splendor.
Virtue/Vice: Truthfulness/Falsehood, Dishonesty.
Titles: The Pentagram, the Lord of Books and Ceremonial Magic.
Symbols: The Caduceus, Names.
Precious Stones: Opal.
Perfume: Storax (liquid amber gum).
Divine Names: Splendor, Glory, Hermes.
Sign of the Cross: None.
Lord's Prayer: Lead us not into Temptation.
Beatitudes: Blessed are they which are persecuted for righteousness' sake ...
Ten Commandments: Thou shall not Steal ...
Hierarchies, Exoteric/Esoteric: Reader (unconscious)/Practicus (conscious).
Seven Sacraments: Confession, Repentance.

YESOD: THE FOUNDATION

Position in the human body: The Genital Organs.
Position in the Temple: The Congregation.
Force: Conception.
Functional Color: Violet.

Name of Power: Shaddai El Chai, Almighty Living One.
Archangel: Gabriel.
Angels: Aishim, Souls of Fire.
Planetary Attribution: The Moon.
Magical Image: A beautiful naked Man, very strong.
Spiritual Experience: Vision of the Machinery of the Universe.
Virtue/Vice: Independence/Idleness.
Titles: Treasure house of Images, the Sphere of Illusion.
Symbols: The Mirror, Perfumes and Sandals.
Precious Stones: Quartz.
Perfume: Jasmine, Ginseng.
Divine Names: Foundation, All Moon Deities.
Sign of the Cross: None. ("And of the Holy Spirit" on the Middle Pillar Cross).
Lord's Prayer: But Deliver us from Evil (Evil One).
Beatitudes: Blessed are ye when men shall revile you and say all manner of evil against you falsely for my sake . . .
Ten Commandments: Thou shall not bear false witness . . .
Hierarchies, Exoteric/Esoteric: Exorcist (unconscious) Theoricus (conscious).
Seven Sacraments: Confirmation, Chrismation.

MALKUTH: THE KINGDOM

Position in the human body: The Feet.
Position in the Temple: Baptismal Font, Entrance Door.
Force: Resolution.
Functional Color: Brown.
Name of Power: Adonai ha Aretz, Lord of the Earth.
Archangel: Sandalphon.
Angels: Kerubim, The Strong.
Planetary Attribution: The Planet Earth.

Magical Image: A young Woman Crowned.

Spiritual Experience: Vision of the Holy Guardian Angel.

Virtue/Vice: Discrimination/Inertia.

Titles: The Gate, the Bride, the Queen.

Symbols: The Altar of the Double Cube, The Magical Circle, The Equal Armed Cross.

Precious Stones: Rock Crystal.

Perfume: Dittany of Crete.

Divine Names: The Kingdom.

Sign of the Cross: None. ("For Thine is the Kingdom" on the Kabalistic Cross.)

Lord's Prayer: For Thine is the Kingdom and the Glory and the Power, of the Father and of the Son, and of the Holy Spirit.

Beatitudes: Rejoice and be exceedingly glad for great is your reward in Heaven . . .

Ten Commandments: Thou shall not covet the Wife or the Possessions of thy Neighbor.

Hierarchies, Exoteric/Esoteric: Door Keeper (unconscious)/Zelator (conscious).

Seven Sacraments: Baptism.

Appendix: E

MEDITATION AND THEURGIC EXERCISES ON THE TREE OF LIFE USING THE FORMULAE OF THE SEVEN FUNDAMENTALS

Many practical exercises and procedures can be used and put together by the Candidate and the members of a Circle of Light Generator to activate the Tree of Life in general and/or one of its Spheres in particular. Consulting well-known books and the Practical Qabalah (such as Dion Fortune's *Mystical Qabalah*, Denning and Phillips' *Magical Philosophy*, and Ellen C. Reed *The Witches' Qabalah*) should make one aware of the traditional approaches.

We are going to add to these by suggesting the correspondences and practical applications resulting from the Seven Fundamentals, or the Master Rituals, which is the original contribution of this work. Moreover, we are going to be as simple, practical, and effective as possible by focusing upon the most important techniques and steps which can then be modified and amplified by the Candidate as he opens up his intuition and makes this work "come alive" for him. For once these methods have become "operational" and the Spheres are "activated" and "alive," they *themselves* will reveal the next step and the more sophisticated developments. There is really no end to the creative experimentation that can be carried out along safe, sound, and effective lines by the Candidate once he has grasped the Fundamentals, mastered the "Tools of the Trade," and succeeded in expanding and transforming his Consciousness. For then a dynamic and creative feedback comes into operation, shedding more light on the Master Rituals and the Tree of Life as these expand and transform the consciousness of the participants.

By way of example, we are going to formulate and analyze two specific exercises: one activating *Hod* and the other *Netzach*, which can then be extended as practical models to the other Sephiroth as well as used alone or in the Circle of Light Generator. At this point it is assumed that to effectively perform such exercises, the basic principles and their practical applications, as outlined in the present book, have been *mastered* and rendered "alive" and "operational" by the Candidate. Specifically:

> **That he has well-understood and is able to utilize the basic tools of the trade, the seven fundamentals, himself and his consciousness, and the basic attributes and correspondences of the spheres of the Tree of Life.**

Please bear in mind, once again, that it is not enough to know the foregoing; to truly make them "come alive" and "speak to us," we must also be able to FEEL THEM, to WILL THEM, to LIVE THEM, and to gradually BECOME THEM!

Activating Hod
Begin with the Opening Phase of the Circle of Light

Generator, either alone or in the actual group (or with any other preparatory technique that will effectively bring about an effort of Introversion, Supraversion, and Infraversion of your attention and psychic energies to then *balance* and *recharge* the Etheric/Physical, Astral, and Mental Bodies, align them properly with your Soul, and circulate the Light, Fire and Life of the Divine Spark in your being).

Continue with the visualization and experience of the Tree of Life in your Aura, putting each Sphere in its right position and with its functional Color. Then activate, a-waken, and lift up the Tree of Life with:

a.   Three Signs of the Cross for AWAKENING,
b.   Three Signs of the Cross for PURIFICATION,
c.   Three Signs of the Cross of CONSECRATION.

Go on using the *Flashing Sword* technique to bring down the Light, Fire and Life into the entire Tree and bring up your Consciousness using the *Rising Serpent* technique to reach the chosen Sephira, *Hod.* Now use the "core muscles of consciousness" to focus your attention and direct your psycho-spiritual energies by *willing, thinking, imagining, intuiting, sensing,* and *experiencing* the following:

a.   **Position in your Body:** Right Hip.
b.   **Functional Color:** Orange
c.   **Name of Power:** Elohim Tzabaoth, God of Hosts.
d.   **Archangels:** Michael
e.   **Magical Image:** A Hermaphrodite or Thoth, Hermes, Lord of Knowledge.
f.   **Virtue/Vice:** Truthfulness/Falsehood, Dishonesty.
g.   **Planetary Attribution:** Mercury.

You can use the four stages of Consciousness expansion upon each of the foregoing, adding or subtracting attributes and correspondences to *Hod* according to inner guidance thus concentrating upon, meditating upon, contemplating, and awakening them theurgically in your being.

At this point you can introduce one or more of the related formulae of the Seven Fundamentals and doing the same with each, that is:

a. **Divine Names:** Splendor, Glory, Thoth, Hermes.
b. **Lord's Prayer:** Lead us not into temptation.
c. **Ten Commandments:** Thou shall not kill.
d. **Beatitudes:** Blessed are they which are persecuted for righteousness sake: for theirs is the Kingdom of Heaven.

Then correlate and integrate all of the foregoing by relating them to: WHAT YOU ARE, THE WAY YOU LIVE, and WHAT YOU WOULD LIKE TO BECOME at *this point* in your life.

What symbols, images, insights, thoughts, feelings, urges, or sensations do you get? Can you effectively evaluate the present functioning of *Hod* in your Tree of Life? Is it overactive or underactive? Do you use *thinking* too much or too little? Or is it properly integrated with *feeling* and the other functions? Are you being *honest* and *truthful* or *dishonest* and *false* with yourself and with others? Can you get Hermes or Thoth to speak to you, to become alive in your being? Can you, at least momentarily, identify with and *become* Hermes or Thoth (or their channel of manifestation in the Three Worlds: Mental, Astral, and Etheric/Physical)? What are the basic Temptations you are now facing? Can you recognize them? Can you overcome them? How and where can you get help to become aware of them and overcome them?

Are you *stealing* something from yourself or others at this point in your life (Money, position, reputation, feelings, insights, ideas, or other)?

Are you being "persecuted for righteousness sake" at

this point in your life? What does this mean to you? If you are, do you have the consciousness and strength to go through this, realizing that it will open a path to achieve spiritual consciousness? Can you transmute negative, destructive suffering into positive, constructive suffering, realizing that suffering can be made into a stepping stone for human and spiritual growth?

Activating Netzach

Begin with the Opening Phase of the Circle of Light Generator either alone or in the actual group (or with another effective preparatory technique).

Continue with the visualization and experience of the Tree of Life in your Aura, putting each Sphere in its right position and with its functional Color. Then activate, awaken, and light up the Tree of Life with:

a. Three Signs of the Cross for AWAKENING,
b. Three Signs of the Cross for PURIFICATION,
c. Three Signs of the Cross of CONSECRATION.

Go on using the *Flashing Sword* technique to bring down the Light, Fire and Life into the entire Tree and bring up your Consciousness using the *Rising Serpent* technique to reach the chosen Sephira, *Netzach*. Now use the "core muscles of consciousness" to focus your attention and direct your psychospiritual energies by *willing, thinking, imagining, intuiting, sensing,* and *experiencing* the following:

a. **Position in your Body:** Left Hip.
b. **Functional Color:** Green
c. **Name of Power:** Yahveh Tzabaoth, Lord of Hosts.
d. **Archangels:** Haniel
e. **Magical Image:** A beautiful naked Woman, Venus, Aphrodite, Goddess of Love.

  f. **Virtue/Vice:** Unselfishness/Unchastity, Lust for Power.
  g. **Planetary Attribution:** Venus.

You can use the four stages of Consciousness expansion upon each of the foreging, adding or subtracting attributes and correspondences to *Netzach* according to inner guidance thus concentrating upon, meditating upon, contemplating, and awakening them theurgically in your being.

At this point you can introduce one or more of the related formulae of the Seven Fundamentals and doing the same with each, that is:

  a. **Divine Names;** Victory, Venus, Aphrodite.
  b. **Lord's Prayer:** Forgive us our trespasses as we forgive those who trespass against us.
  c. **Ten Commandments:** Thou shall not commit adultery.
  d. **Beatitudes:** Blessed are the peacemakers: for they shall be called the children of God.

Then correlate and integrate all of the foregoing by relating them to: WHAT YOU ARE, THE WAY YOU LIVE, and WHAT YOU WOULD LIKE TO BECOME at *this point* in your life.

What symbols, images, insights, thoughts, feelings, urges, or sensations do you get? Can you effectively evaluate the present functioning of *Netzach* in your Tree of Life? Is it overactive or underactive? Do you use *feeling* too much or too little? Or is it properly integrated with *thinking* and the other functions? Are you being *selfish* or *unselfish* with yourself and with others? Do you have a *"lust for power"* or are you *unchaste*? What does this mean to you? What *Victory* can you experience in your life, being, and those of others? Can you get Venus or Aphrodite to speak to you, to become alive in your being? Can you, at least momentarily, identify with and *become* Venus or Aphrodite (or their channel of manifestation in the Three Worlds)?

Are you able to forgive yourself and others for imperfections, mistakes, and hurts? Do you know what forgiveness is and can you practice it regularly?

Are you committing *adultery* at this point in your life (taking something or appropriating something which is really not yours, not wanted by your Higher Self)? Can you recognize Adultery and overcome it?

Are you being a "peacemaker" at this point in your life? What does this mean to you? If you are, are you aware of how this attitude and response to life makes you a child of God? Can you objectively bring peace and harmony to yourself, to your conscience, and to others you interact with?

One of the major Principles of Qabalistic Operation and of the Great Work is to reconcile opposites or synthesize opposed energies, tendencies, and elements in your being. Specifically, on the Tree of Life, this means to find the proper equilibrium between

> **Hod and Netzach: Thinking and Feeling, Separating and Combining.**
> **Geburah and Chesed: Severity and Mercy, Energy and Order.**
> **Binah and Chokmah: Understanding and Wisdom, Contraction and Expansion.**

Can you, personally, apply this to your *Hod* and *Netzach*?

> Valuable "thought seeds" to achieve the above are:
> "Hod is the text of a ritual, the form, while Netzach is the performace of the ritual and the energy given to it."

> "Hod is the drawn pentagam; Netzach, the flame

when it is charged."

"Netzach is sound. Hod is words, sound in pattern."

"Netzach is concerned with Nature contact and elemental contacts; Hod with ritual magic and knowledge for the sake of knowledge."

"Hod is the Lord of Books; Netzach the Lady of Nature. Hod is instinct; Netzach, emotion. Hod is Ceremonial Magic; Netzach, the traditional Craft."

STAY IN TOUCH

On the following pages you will find listed, with their current prices, some of the books and tapes now available on related subjects. Your book dealer stocks most of these, and will stock new titles in the Llewellyn series as they become available. We urge your patronage.

However, to obtain our full catalog, to keep informed of new titles as they are released and to benefit from informative articles and helpful news, you are invited to write for our bi-monthly news magazine/catalog. A sample copy is free, and it will continue coming to you at no cost as long as you are an active mail customer. Or you may keep it coming for a full year with a donation of just $2.00 in U.S.A. ($7.00 for Canada & Mexico, $10.00 overseas, first class mail). Many bookstores also have *The Llewellyn New Times* available to their customers. Ask for it.

Stay in touch! In *The Llewellyn New Times'* pages you will find news and reviews of new books, tapes and services, announcements of meetings and seminars, articles helpful to our readers, news of authors, advertising of products and services, special money-making opportunities, and much more.

The Llewellyn New Times
P.O. Box 64383-Dept. 676, St. Paul, MN 55164-0383, U.S.A.

•   •   •

TO ORDER BOOKS AND TAPES

If your book dealer does not have the books and tapes described on the following pages readily available, you may order them direct from the publisher by sending full price in U.S. funds, plus $1.00 for handling and 50¢ each book or item for postage within the United States; outside USA surface mail add $1.00 extra per item. Outside USA air mail add $7.00 per item.

FOR GROUP STUDY AND PURCHASE

Because there is a great deal of interest in group discussion and study of the subject matter of this book, we feel that we should encourage the adoption and use of this particular book by such groups by offering a special "quantity" price to group leaders or "agents".

Our Special Quality Price for a minimum order of five copies of THE INVISIBLE TEMPLE is $29.85 Cash-With-Order. This price includes postage and handling within the United States. Minnesota residents must add 6% sales tax. For additional quantities, please order in multiples of five. For Canadian and foreign orders, add postage and handling charges as above. Credit Card (VISA, MasterCard, American Express, Diners' Club) Orders are accepted. Charge Card Orders only may be phoned free ($15.00 minimum order) within the U.S.A. by dialing 1-800-THE MOON (in Canada call: 1-800-FOR-SELF). Customer Service calls dial 1-612-291-1970 and ask for "Kae". Mail Orders to:

LLEWELLYN PUBLICATIONS
P.O. Box 64383-Dept. 676 / St. Paul, MN 55164-0383, U.S.A.

THE NATURE AND USE OF RITUAL
by Dr. Peter Roche de Coppens

The New Age is not a time or place, but a *new state of consciousness*. To bring about this new consciousness, we need a viable source of revelation and teaching that gets to the heart of our Being and Reality: a way of living and seeing that leads to a gradual, organic and holistic (or 'holy') transformation of the present consciousness and being.

The basic aim of this book is to render explicit the essence of this process of *bio-psycho-spiritual* transformation in terms of our own indigenous Spiritual Tradition, which we can find in the very basic Christian Prayers and Documents.

Perhaps at no time in history has the need for new consciousness been greater — if indeed we are to survive and fulfill our destiny and the Divine potential that is seeded within each person.

At no time has the opportunity been greater, for access to the highest esoteric knowledge, the most refined spiritual technology, is now available to bring about the transformation of consciousness on a massive scale—only if each of us accepts this goal as our personal responsibility.

0-87542-675-1, 229 pages, softcover, illus. **$9.95**

THE ODES OF SOLOMON
by Robert Winterhalter

Original Christianity revealed! 42 powerful tools for spiritual and material well-being are included in this revolutionary book.

Think about it: If God made human beings in "His Image," we certainly do not expect that God "looks" like you or I or even George Burns! The Bible says "in Him we live and move and have our being" (Acts 17:28) and Jesus said "he who believes in me will also do the works I do" (John 14:12). The Kingdom of God is within you (Luke 17:21) must mean exactly that! Within each of us sleeps a Divine Spark which, when awakened, brings the realization of "God as source of our very being" with the ability to bring God-power into our lives!

Cane *we* deny this obvious meaning? What Jesus taught was THE WAY to that realization, and now these teachings have been recovered in this First Century document, and combined into a modern easy to use and understand process—*as it was practiced in Jesus' time*—to bring Christ Consciousness and God-p;ower into your own life *with all the benefits that implies!*

0-87542-875-4, 288 pages 5¼ x 8, softcover **$9.95**

THE LLEWELLYN PRACTICAL GUIDES
by Melita Denning & Osborne Phillips

THE LLEWELLYN PRACTICAL GUIDE TO ASTRAL PROJECTION.
Yes, your consciousness can be sent forth, out-of-the-body, with full awareness and return with full memory. You can travel through time and space, converse with non-physical entities, obtain knowledge by non-material means, and experience higher dimensions.

> Is there life-after-death? Are we forever shackled by Time & Space? The ability to go forth by means of the Astral Body, or Body of Light, gives the personal assurance of consciousness (and life) beyond the limitations of the physical body. No other answer to these ageless questions is as meaningful as experienced reality.

The reader is led through the essential stages for the inner growth and development that will culminate in fully conscious projection and return. Not only are the requisite practices set forth in step-by-step procedures, augmented with photographs and puts-you-in-the-picture" visualization aids, but the vital reasons for undertaking them are clearly explained. Beyond this, the great benefits from the various practices themselves are demonstrated in renewed physical and emotional health, mental discipline, spiritual attainment, and the development of extra faculties".

Guidance is also given to the Astral World itself: what to expect, what can be done—including the ecstatic experience of Astral Sex between two people who project together into this higher world where true union is consumated free of the barriers of physical bodies.

0-87542-181-4, 239 pages, 5¼ x 8, softcover **$7.95**

SUPPLEMENTAL DEEP MIND TAPE

THE LLEWELLYN DEEP MIND TAPE FOR ASTRAL PROJECTION.
This is a tool so powerful that it is offered only for use in conjunction with the above book. The authors of this book are adepts fully experienced in all levels of psychic development and training, and have designed this 90-minute cassette tape to guide the student through full relaxation and all the preparations for projection, and then—with the added dimension of the authors personally produced electronic synthesizer patterns of sound and music—they program the Deep Mind through the stages of awakening, and projection of, the astral Body of Light. And then the programming guides your safe return to normal consciousness with memory—enabling you to bridge the worlds of Body, Mind and Spirit.

> The Deep Mind Tape is a powerful new technique combining guided Mind Programming with specially created sound and music to evoke deep level response in the psyche and its psychic centres for controlled development, and induction of the OUT-OF-BODY EXPERIENCE.

0-87542-168-7, 90-minute cassette tape. **$9.95**

Note: If you have the book, THE LLEWELLYN PRACTICAL GUIDE TO ASTRAL PROJECTION, you may order this DEEP MIND TAPE by sending full price, plus $1.50 postage & handling ($7.00 overseas airmail). Or, you can order both Book AND Tape for a special price of just $15.00 Postpaid in U.S.A. ($25.00 overseas airmail).

THE LLEWELLYN PRACTICAL GUIDE TO CREATIVE VISUALIZATION.
All things you will ever want must have their start in your mind. The average person uses very little of the full creative power that is his, potentially. It's like the power locked in the atom—it's all there, but you have to learn to release it and apply it constructively.

> **IF YOU CAN SEE IT . . . in your Mind's Eye . . . you will have it! It's true: you can have whatever you want—but there are "laws" to Mental Creation that must be followed. The power of the mind is not limited to, nor limited by, the Material World—Creative Visualization enables Man to reach beyond, into the Invisible World of Astral and Spiritual Forces.**

Some people apply this innate power without actually knowing what they are doing, and achieve great success and happiness; most people, however, use this same power, again unknowingly, INCORRECTLY, and experience bad luck, failure, or at best unfulfilled life.
This book changes that. Through an easy series of step-by-step, progressive exercises, your mind is applied to bring desire into realization! Wealth, Power, Success, Happiness . . . even Psychic Powers . . . even what we call Magickal Power and Spiritual Attainment . . . all can be yours. You can easily develop this completely natural power, and correctly apply it, for your immediate and practical benefit. Illustrated with unique, "puts-you-into-the-picture" visualization aids.

0-87542-183-0, 255 pages, 5¼ x 8, softcover.   **$7.95**

THE LLEWELLYN PRACTICAL GUIDE TO THE DEVELOPMENT OF PSYCHIC POWERS. You may not realize it, but . . . you already have the ability to use ESP, Astral Vision and Clairvoyance, Divination, Dowsing, Prophecy, Communications with Spirits, Mental Telepathy, etc. WE ALL HAVE THESE POWERS! It's simply a matter of knowing what to do, and then to exercise (as with any talent) and develop them.

Written by two of the most knowledgeable experts in the world of Magick today, this book is a complete course—teaching you, step-by-step, how to develop these powers that actually have been yours since birth. Using the techniques they teach, you will soon be able to move objects at a distance, see into the future, know the thoughts and feelings of another person, find lost objects, locate water and even people using your own no-longer latent talents.

Psychic powers are as much a natural ability as any other talent. You'll learn to play with those new skills, work with groups of friends to accomplish things you never would have believed possible before reading this book. The text shows you how to make the equipment you can use, the exercises you can do—many of them at any time, anywhere—and how to use your abilities to change your life and the lives of those close to you. Many of the exercises are presented in forms that can be adapted as games for pleasure and fun, as well as development. Illustrated throughout.

0-87542-191-1, 244 pages, 5¼ x 8, softcover.   **$7.95**

THE LLEWELLYN PRACTICAL GUIDE TO PSYCHIC SELF-DEFENSE AND WELL-BEING. Psychic Well-Being and Psychic Self-Defense are two sides of the same coin—just as physical health and resistance to disease are:

> **FACT: Each person (and every living thing) is surrounded by an electro-magnetic Force Field, or AURA, that can provide the means to Psychic Self-Defense and to dynamic Well-Being.**

This book explores the world of very real "psychic warfare" that we all are victims of:

> **FACT: Every person in our modern world is subjected, constantly, to psychic stress and psychological bombardment: advertising and sales promotions that play upon primitive emotions, political and religious appeals that work on feelings of insecurity and guilt, noise, threats of violence and war, news of crime and disaster, etc.**

This book shows the nature of genuine psychic attacks—ranging from actual acts of black magic to bitter jealousy and hate—and the reality of psychic stress, the structure of the psyche and its interrelationship with the physical body. It shows how each person must develop his weakened aura into a powerful defense-shield—thereby gaining both physical protection and energetic well-being that can extend to protection from physical violence, accidents . . . even ill-health.

This book gives exact instructions for the fortification of the aura, specific techniques for protection, and the Rite of the First Kathisma using the PSALMS to invoke Divine Blessing. Illustrated with "puts-you-into-the-picture" drawings, and includes powerful techniques not only for your personal use but for group use.

0-87542-190-3, 277 pages, 5¼ x 8, softcover. $7.95

THE LLEWELLYN PRACTICAL GUIDE TO THE MAGICK OF THE TAROT. *How to Read, And Shape, Your Future.*

"To gain understanding, *and control*, of Your Life."—Can anything be more important? To gain insight into the circumstances of your life—the inner causes, the karmic needs, the hidden factors at work—and then to have the power to change your life in order to fulfill your real desires and True Will: that's what the techniques taught in this book can do.

Discover the Shadows cast ahead by Coming Events.

Yes, this is possible, because it is your DEEP MIND—that part of your psyche, normally beyond your conscious awareness, which is in touch with the World Soul and with your own Higher (and Divine) Self—that perceives the *astral shadows* of coming events and can communicate them to you through the symbols and images of the ancient and mysterious Tarot Cards.

This book teaches you both how to read the Tarot Cards: seeing the likely outcome of the present trends and the hidden forces now at work shaping tomorrow's circumstances, and then—as never before presented to the public—how you can expand this same system to bring these causal forces under your conscious control.

0-87542-198-9, 252 pages, 5¼ x 8, illust., softcover. $7.95

MAGICAL STATES OF CONSCIOUSNESS
by Melita Denning and Osborne Phillips

Magical States of Consciousness are dimensions of the Human Psyche giving us access to the knowledge and powers of the Great Archetypes. These dimensions are attained as we travel the Paths of the Qabalah's Tree of Life—that "blueprint" to the structure of the Lesser Universe of the Human Psyche and to the Greater Universe in which we have our being.

Published here for the first time are not only the complete texts for these inward journeys to the Deep Unconscious Mind, but complete guidance to their application in Spiritual Growth and Initiation, Psychological Integration and "Soul Sculpture" (the secret technique by which we may shape our own character). Here, too, are *Magical Mandalas* for each of the Path-Workings that serve as "doorways" to altered states of consciousness when used with the Path-Working narrations, and *Magical Images* of the Sephirothic Archetypes as used in invoking those powerful forces.

0-87542-194-6, 420 pages, Illust.,softcover. $12.95

THE LLEWELLYN INNER GUIDE TAPES

Each tape is accompanied by a booklet of necessary instructions, with the appropriate Magical Mandala for the path being worked.

All tapes are $9.95 each

32nd Path: Governing Intelligence, Development of intuition, enhance astral projection, and creative visualization. **0-87542-151-2**

31st Path: Unresting Intelligence

30th Path: Collating Intelligence, 31st Path develops courage, enhances past life recall, arouses Kundalini, frees you from emotional conditioning. 30th Path enhances healing powers, develops discipline, assists in visualization operations. **0-87542-152-0**

29th Path: The Bodily Intelligence

28th Path: The Perfecting Intelligence, 29th Path spreads harmony, heals family disputes, assists with helping animals, increases prosperity, enhances scrying. 28th Path disciplines the mind, helps in astrological analysis, planning career. **0-87542-153-9**

27th Path: Awakening Intelligence, Courage to face fears, skill in avoiding quarrels, banishing in magical rites, love. **0-87542-154-7**

26th Path, Part I: The Renewing Intelligence

24th Path, Part 1: Image-making Intelligence, Preparing for transformation, the 26th Path asks why caution prosperity, sexuality, and goodness? The 24th Path queries Death. **0-87542-155-5**

25th Path: Critical Intelligence, Strengthens bonds with Higher Self, develops self-confidence, assists in calling up God Forms, astral projection, invoking HGA. Protection while traveling. **0-87542-156-3**

26th Path, Part 2: Gives access to inner powers and outer control over tendency to domineer. Used for exorcism, rites of protection for home. Promotes generosity and tolerance. **0-87542-157-1**

24th Path, Part 2:
24th Path assuages grief, resolves inner conflicts. Used for Sex Magick, helps in understanding adolescents, **0-87542-158-X**

MYSTERIA MAGICA
(formerly Volume V of the Magical Philosophy Series)
by Melita Denning and Osborne Phillips

THE INNER SECRETS REVEALED: The Secret Symbolism of the Aurum Solis is given to you for the first time! The Gates to Knowledge, Ecstasy, and Power are opened to give modern man powers undreamed of in past ages. For those who would know the Meaning of their lives, who do know that we are more than simple machines, who believe—and would experience—there is Beauty and Love in the Universe.

> No matter what your level of ability in Ceremonial Magick, this is one of the most important books you could ever own. Bringing together the best of the magical systems of Egypt, Ireland, Pre-Columbian America, the Mediterranian, Northern Europe and the Middle East, the authors lead us into new and profound areas of Magical Work. Knowledge is power, and the knowledge presented in these pages is some of the most powerful ever published.

". . . Whatever forms exoteric religion may have taken, the Western approach to life has always been active and practical. There is, as we recognize, a great body of magical knowledge, which as a means of attainment is worthy to take its place among the great mystical systems of the world; its neglect hitherto by so many serious scholars must be attributed to its wide scope and the multiplicity of its levels, as well as to the atmosphere of secrecy with which in many lands and ages it has been surrounded."

> MYSTERIA MAGICA offers you essential and profound magical knowledge, authentic texts and formulae of the Western Mystery Tradition which have hitherto been hidden in inaccessible libraries, in enigmatic writings, or in rarely-imparted teachings passed on only by word of mouth; and, in addition, it contains ample sections showing you how to use all that is disclosed, how to give potent consecration to your own magical weapons, how to build rites on the physical and astral planes with word and action, sound, color and visualization, to implement your own magical will.

Here are secrets which have been guarded through centuries by an elite among popes and rabbis, adepts and seers, dervishes and mages. Here, explicitly set forth, is knowledge by which the mystical priesthood of Egypt wielded true God-force through millennia, thaumaturgist in establishing bonds of knowledge, love and power with their chosen deific force however named.

> The setting of the Wards of Power (Greek and Hebrew forms); The Setting of the Wards of Adamant (Sub Rosa Nigra); the Clavis Rei Primae and Orante Formulae; Banishing and Invoking; Identifying with God-forces; Rising on the Planes; Astral Projection; Works undertaken through Astral Projection; Formula of the Watcher; Elementary techniques of Scrying; The Constellation of the Worshipped; Principles of Ceremonial; The Dance as Instrument of Magick; Images; Sigils; Conjurations of the Art; Enochian Studies (Text and Commentaries); Consecrations and the Use of the Magical Weapons; Sphere-Working; Evocation to Visible Appearance; Transubstantiation; Consecration of a Talisman; and much more—with tables, guidance to pronunciation of Enochian, workings with Elementals, formulae for integration, etc.

0-87542-196-2, 450 pages, revised, softcover. $15.00

THE INNER WORLD OF FITNESS
Melita Denning

Because the artificialities and the daily hassles of routine living tend to turn our attention from the real values, *The Inner World of Fitness* leads us back by means of those natural factors in life which remain to us: air, water, sunlight, the food we eat, the world of nature, meditation, sexual love and the power of our own wishes—so that through these things we can re-link ourselves in awareness to the great non-material forces of life and of being which underlie them.

The unity and interaction of inner and outer, keeping body and psyche open to the great currents of life and of the natural forces, is seen as the essential secret of *youthfulness* and hence of radiant fitness. Regardless of our physical age, so long as we are within the flow of these great currents, we have the vital quality of youthfulness: but if we begin to close off or turn away from those contacts, in the same measure we begin to lose youthfulness.

0-87542-165-2, 240 pgs., 5¼ x 8, softcover. $7.95

METAPHYSICS:
THE SCIENCE OF LIFE
by Anthony J. Fisichella

There are thousands of books and articles on "metaphysical" subjects, such as the meaning of life, the nature of God, the teachings of various religions, reincarnation, life after death, the various disciplines such as astrology, numerology, tarot, ESP research, healing, and many others. Is there a "golden thread of wisdom" which encompasses a broad-based understanding of the essential truths of the various teachings? Is there a primer where one can learn the fundamental concepts, the common denominator present in most spiritual teachings?

There is now, in Tony Fisichella's **METAPHYSICS: THE SCIENCE OF LIFE.** For the first time, here is one book which ties together the ancient and modern teachings about human life—which answers the basic questions that most thinking people ask: who am I, where did I come from, what am I here for, where am I going? Here is a book which can change your way of thinking, which can provide the reference you need to help solve practical problems, to find the direction you seek, to understand the teachings of great relgions in their true context. Here is a book which can truly change your life.

0-87542-229-2, 300 pages, illus., softcover. $9.95

THE LLEWELLYN ANNUALS

Llewellyn's MOON SIGN BOOK: approximately 400 pages of valuable information on gardening, fishing, weather, stock market forecasts, personal horoscopes, good planting dates, and general instructions for finding the best date to do just about anything! Articles by prominent forecasters and writers in the fields of gardening, astrology, politics, economics and cycles. This special almanac, different from any other, has been published annually since 1906. It's fun, informative and has been a great help to millions in their daily planning.

State year $3.95

Llewellyn's SUN SIGN BOOK: Your personal horoscope for the entire year! All 12 signs are included in one handy book. Also included are political and economic forecasts, special feature articles, and lucky dates for each sign. Monthly horoscopes by a prominent radio and TV astrologer for your personal Sun Sign. Articles on a variety of subjects written by well-known astrologers from around the country. Much more than just a horoscope guide! Entertaining and fun the year round.

State year $3.95

Llewellyn's DAILY PLANETARY GUIDE and ASTROLOGER'S DATE-BOOK: Includes all of the major daily aspects plus their exact times in Eastern and Pacific time zones, lunar phases, signs and voids plus their times, planetary motion, a monthly ephemeris, sunrise and sunset tables, special articles on the planets, signs, aspects, a business guide, planetary hours, rulerships, and much more. Large 5¼ × 8 format for more writing space, spiral bound to lay flat, address and phone listings, time zone conversion chart and blank horoscope chart.   **State year $5.95**

Llewellyn's ASTROLOGICAL CALENDAR: Large wall calendar of 52 pages. Beautiful full color cover and color inside. Includes special feature articles by famous astrologers, introductory information on astrology, Lunar Gardening Guide, celestial phenomena for the year, a blank horoscope chart for your own chart data, and monthly date pages which include aspects, lunar information, planetary motion, ephemeris, personal forecasts, lucky dates, planting and fishing dates, and more. 10 x 13 size. Set in Central time, with conversion table for other time zones worldwide.

State year $6.95